THE WAR ON WISDOM

We acknowledge the permission of A P Watt Ltd on behalf of Michael B Yeats to reproduce stanzas from An Acre of Grass and Sailing to Byzantium from W B Yeats' Collected Poems and of Faber & Faber to reproduce stanzas from The Old Fools and Aubade from Philip Larkin's Collected Poems

THE WAR ON
WISDOM

WISDOM VERSUS EXPERTISE
IN FACING
LIFE'S PROBLEMS

EDITED BY
DIGBY ANDERSON

THE SOCIAL AFFAIRS UNIT

Published by the Social Affairs Unit

British Library Cataloguing in Publication Data
A catalogue record of this book is available from
The British Library

ISBN 0 90763198 3

The Social Affairs Unit gratefully acknowledges support received
from the following foundations during the course of this project: The
Charlotte and Walter Kohler Charitable Trust, The Daily Telegraph
Charitable Trust and The Garfield Weston Foundation.

Printed by St. Edmundsbury Press
Bury St. Edmunds, Suffolk

Contents

The authors

Dr Digby Anderson is Director of the Social Affairs Unit.

Dr Jon Davies formerly taught in the Department of Religious Studies, University of Newcastle upon Tyne.

Professor John Danford is Professor of Political Science at Loyola University, Chicago.

Dr Karen Danford teaches at the University of Chicago. The Danfords have three children.

Dr Robert Grant is Reader in English, University of Glasgow.

Dr Simon Green is a Fellow and Sub-Warden of All Souls College, Oxford and Senior Lecturer in Modern History at the University of Leeds.

Rabbi Daniel Lapin is President of Toward Tradition and founding rabbi of Pacific Jewish Center, Venice, California.

Dr Athena S Leoussi is a lecturer in sociology, University of Reading.

Revd Peter Mullen is rector of St Michael's, Cornhill in the City of London.

Professor Graeme Newman is Professor of Criminal Justice, University of Albany, New York.

Dr Lucy Sullivan is an independent social and political analyst and demographer. She is currently working on low fertility rates for the Menzies Research Centre in Canberra.

Dr Carolyn Womersley is a general practitioner in Oxford.

Dr David Womersley is a Fellow of Jesus College, Oxford.

Wisdom versus expertise in facing life's problems

Digby Anderson

How much longer can Western civilization last? For surely some day it must fall as all the other great civilizations – Greek, Roman, Chinese – have fallen. What built this civilization and sustains it is knowledge. Civilizations are built on knowledge, knowledge about war, about keeping order, about innovation, agriculture, about the arts and the moral life too. This knowledge is more than facts; it involves also some sort of commitment to and institutionalisation of understanding. What, more precisely, is this knowledge on which our order and civilization depend: and which, if forgotten, spurned or lost will cause it to fall?

The peoples of rich and successful countries such as Britain and the United States are truly fortunate though not noticeably grateful for their good fortune. Most have their material needs satisfied. They have long lives and considerable freedom. These benefits are the result, in large part, of enormous progress in certain sorts of knowledge, especially scientific and technological expertise and advances in political constitutions and market order. All this happy progress, however, still leaves plenty of problems to be anxious and miserable about. Marriages[1] collapse in bitterness and recrimination. Parents have difficulties with their children and children with parents. Surveys show we value friendship highly but we are not as good, may even be worse at making and keeping friends as past societies. Millions find their work unsatisfying. Less obviously, perhaps, many find their play, their leisure, games and the arts not so reliably rewarding as they would hope. Despite the riches and the huge expenditure of welfare states, the poor remain obstinately with us and we don't seem to have found efficient ways of helping them. In the UK, despite these huge amounts, the poverty lobby alleges that poverty has even increased. In the USA, one aptly titled account of the war on poverty was a book called *Losing Ground*.[2] The criminals certainly remain with us and we are even less effective at dealing with them than with the poor. Indeed less so than earlier societies: the Victorians halved the crime rate over the last fifty years of the nineteenth century. Modern society, with all its academic theories, tested evidence, scientific criminological research and technically equipped policing, has seen crime more or less remorselessly rise.

The diseases we suffer from and die from have changed. Tuberculosis and childhood diseases have been largely defeated. Heart disease is being reduced. But we still have to suffer from diseases. Indeed our success in defeating old diseases and lengthening life opens the way for a whole series of new diseases, those of senescence. If the diseased themselves still suffer, so do the families of those who are afflicted by, say, Alzheimer's. We still have to get old with the problems that brings, indeed we are old for longer now. We still have, however belatedly, to die. And before that we have to deal with the deaths of those we love.

These are the perennial problems. Unlike some of the problems of wealth creation and extension of life through medical advance, they are not solely or largely technical. These problems have something to do with what it means to be human. The sort of knowledge that helps create wealth, expertise, does not seem very effective at banishing loneliness or making us better parents or patients. Indeed an excessive and misplaced expectation of what expertise can deliver in these matters, for instance in medicine, can result in disappointment, resentment and litigation.

Yet there is a knowledge, another sort of knowledge that speaks to the human problems. It is called wisdom. Just as the problems of loneliness, marital strife and betrayed friendship are not new, so the wisdom comes from the past. There is a lot of the past and thus a lot of wisdom. It is the accumulated thought, the best that people have been able to think. It is found in the great books of Athens and Rome, in the Bible, in Shakespeare, in novels, children's tales, epigrams and proverbs.

It is often startling. Thus traditional wisdom about illness[3] questions our modern understanding when it suggests that ill-health is not entirely to be regretted or feared. As the word, patient, suggests, wisdom unlike misplaced technical knowledge teaches patience in sickness and gratitude for health. Being ill shows us our true friends and what really matters. There's nothing like a severe illness in ourselves or those we love to show us how trivial are the things we used to worry about before. It teaches fortitude. John Donne points out that what is worst in illness is not pain but the danger of being separated from the mainstream of the lives of the healthy:

As Sicknesse is the greatest misery, so the greatest misery of sicknes is solitude; when the infectiousness of the disease deterrs them who should assist, from coming...Solitude is a torment, which is not threatned in hell it selfe.[4]

Traditional wisdom about friendship is similarly startling. The modern age is one which encourages cults of fame, celebrity and attention. Yet Greek and Roman wisdom about friendship[5] warns us not to confuse it with flattery. It is a friend's duty to tell you the truth about yourself:

Speak as boldly with [your friend] as with yourself...Share with him at least all your worries and reflections...Why need I keep back any words in the presence of a friend?[6]

Traditional wisdom can be startling

Modern knowledge thinks friendship is enjoying a drink together and a game of golf, perhaps sharing the odd confidence. Classical wisdom makes friendship both wider and deeper. It is a moral relationship in which two friends bring out the morally best in each other, rather like a good marriage, indeed say the Greeks, as or more important than marriage: and something not private but necessary for the good society. Aristotle says,

Only the friendship of those who are good and similar in their goodness, is perfect"[7]

Cicero says friendship is,

Complete identity of feeling about all things divine and human, as strengthened by mutual goodwill and affection[8]

Friendship, then, should be ennobling – a word we find difficult to understand. So should another part of daily life, that of work. Our current preoccupations with finding well-paid work, getting our "rights" as employees, expecting a job to suit us, are a million miles from the understanding of work in, say, the book of *Proverbs*[9]. Consider what the world would be like without work, deserts, forests, wild elements, no shelter, violent, hungry, nasty, brutish and short. The order we see and expect about us is the fruit of work. Work is how human beings keep chaos at bay. And if that is a striking because so unexpected an observation, other Proverbs disconcert because they literally disturb us, for instance Proverbs about work directed at "sluggards" are remarkable in condemning what we should regard as a well-earned rest, "time-out" or the benefits of relaxing as sloth. In yet other cases, wisdom says not so much something different from contemporary knowledge but says it so much better.

Classical wisdom catches the good side of old age well[10], how losing physical appetites may be a liberation from "mad and furious masters". Losing some of the sex drive or greed for material things and the impulse to show off and create effects may enhance a properly human life not diminish it. Wisdom understood how the old should be respected and deserve a special place in society reserved for them by nature, how, as with other ages, it is character which determines whether growing old will be good or bad.

When wisdom startles modern sensibilities, it does so partly because it is so seldom heard. Neither Latin nor Greek authors nor the Bible occupy the place they did in modern education and even less in modern homes. Wisdom comes from the past and the modern age is an arrogant one which thinks it has nothing to learn from the past. This may indeed be true in certain disciplines, especially the sciences where any modern knows far more than past scientists. It is not true of philosophy, theology and the arts where questions are not so much to be answered but reflected on, where the crucial thing is what they do to the questioner and where moderns may be less competent and sensible than Aristotle or the author of *Proverbs*.

Wisdom about marriage, welfare and crime is an obstacle for modern projects

Today, there are also those who fear what wisdom teaches. For instance, Christian wisdom sustained a certain high, demanding understanding of marriage for more than a thousand years.[11] It was written into law. It demanded of the marriage partners love, not so much falling in love but sustained love, honour, unselfish support, companionship, procreation, the pursuit of virtue by parents and children and constant fidelity and trust. Most awkward of all, wisdom said that a married couple became one and should remain one for ever. Marriage was indissoluble. It was a conception of marriage which was, at the least, inconvenient and restrictive to certain persons' desires. The modern reaction to this wisdom was certainly not to neglect or forget it, but to deride it as "just a piece of paper", or as inconveniently restrictive of the ambitions of romantic love and sex. In consequence modernity fought wisdom. There has been a war against marriage wisdom and, with the acceptance of no fault divorce and marriage seen as whatever arrangement suits the two participants, wisdom has lost the war.

The war against wisdom has been fought on other fronts, notably the upbringing of children where wisdom saw children as savages to be tamed and disciplined into civilized life and progressive thought saw them as innocents whose whims are to be indulged.[12] A similar war was fought more generally over punishment, especially over punishment of children. Another was fought over the punishment of criminals[13] and yet another over welfare. Wisdom saw welfare as a complicated affair.[14] It depended on finding out exactly who was in need, what they needed, what sort of assistance might help them to a better life and what might trap them in dependence. Traditional thinking about charity believed in being close to the person in need and distinguishing among those asking for welfare. The modern view is that the needy require efficient, computerized delivery systems via which the state grants standard handouts to huge classes of people without interest in their particular circumstances.

This reliance on lumping individuals together so that they can be solved by expertly designed systems is paradoxically accompanied by a massive diet of sentimentality in which uncomfortable aspects of human nature are ignored. Wisdom was far more realistic even when it was cast in what looked like simple, innocent children's tales. Aesop tells of the farmer who, one winter, found a snake stiff with cold. He placed it under his shirt and warmed it against his chest. The snake revived, struck out and killed his benefactor. Dying, the man said, "I well deserve it for taking pity on a wicked wretch". As the commentators to the tale add, "The perversity of nature does not change under the influence of kindness".[15] Another tale is of the son who steals a writing tablet from school and gives it to his mother who accepts it. Later he steals other, more expensive things and is sentenced to execution. His mother comes to him in tears. He asks her to come close so he can whisper something in her ear before he dies. She does so and he bites off his mother's ear, "If you had thrashed me the first time I brought home the stolen writing tablet, I would not now be facing death".[16] They shock because modern knowledge refuses to acknowledge the power of evil and its rootedness in human nature. It thinks it can easily and gently make bad people good and is averse to punishment especially physical punishment. The consequence of this spurning of wisdom is a soaring crime rate, a recidivism rate of 70 per cent and widespread disorder, violence and vandalism in public places, especially where order, quiet and peacefulness should reign such as classrooms, hospitals and churches.

Isolating and ignoring wisdom about friendship and work

On other fronts, progressives have preferred to isolate wisdom, not to mention it and hope that it will be forgotten. That is the case with friendship. With the slightest of exceptions no notable book has been written on friendship for 300 years. Classical philosophers such as Aristotle and Cicero gave it pride of place. You won't find a mention, still less a chapter on it in most modern philosophy books. While the Bible is full of references to friendship and it is exalted by Christ – "I call you friends – Greater love hath no man than this, that he lay down his life for his friends", the modern church has nothing to say about it. Compare the vast references to the family with this wilful neglect of friendship. The same is true about wisdom on work. If it is not used as an excuse to go on about rights, it is usually ignored. If wisdom about growing old has attracted neither attack nor scorn, that is largely because the old are themselves not regarded as persons of importance by those designing the march to an exciting future.

Ignoring wisdom about the arts, games, illness and growing old

Derision, bluster and the lauding of technique and performance are used to dismiss wisdom about games, that old amateur spirit which saw them as part of character, and replace it with a professionalism obsessed with winning, performance and equipment, with "expertise".[17] Imagine the contempt that would be poured on anyone these days who took seriously P G Wodehouse's rather nice remark,

> Golf...is the infallible test [of a man's character]. The man who can go into a patch of rough alone, with the knowledge that only God is watching him, and play his ball wherever it lies, is a man who will serve you faithfully and well.[18]

In the visual arts, wisdom taught that art was essentially tied up with beauty and goodness.[19] Modern art with its values of shocking people and being subversive, its obsession with form disconnected from humanity, has broken this essential link. Yet, as recent and "modern" a painter as Matisse could still write in 1908,

> What I dream of is an art of balance, purity and serenity devoid of troubling or depressing subject matter...a soothing, calming influence on the mind, rather like a good armchair which provides relaxation from physical fatigue.[20]

With sickness and death, progressivism has simply changed the subject. There is an enormous interest in health in modern society both science-based medicine and witch-doctory alternative health. Some of it is positive for science-based medicine has indeed postponed death. But much of it is an attempt to divert attention from the inescapable facts that curing one disease merely extends life for another to arrive and that death is inevitable. Modern society needs an Isaiah to tell it, as he did Hezekiah, "thus saith the Lord, Set thy house in order, for thou shalt die, and not live".[21] Not to face illness and death is to live a lie, a childish evasion. No traditional wisdom would countenance such evasion.

Wisdom is resented because it tells uncomfortable truths and in demanding forms

This explains the reason for the war on wisdom. It proclaims uncomfortable truths. It reminds us of what it is to be weak, wicked and mortal humans. It also reminds us in forms which the modern sensibility is impatient with or resents. I thought, starting on this book that in wisdom there would be lots of neat two line gems on marriage, sickness, work and the other perennial troubles of life. There are, and many will be found in the pages that follow. But even the proverbs and epigrams say little unless the reader is prepared to learn. Wisdom is associated often with "secrets". To understand the secrets in the two-liners you have to want to learn. You have to understand the tradition in which the saying is said – more, you have to become part of the tradition in which the saying is said. The Proverbs are not only words of the wise but "words to the wise". You have to be prepared to accept the frequent rebuking character of wisdom. For instance, Christ's replies to questions very often involve rebuking the questioner and the audience; "You hypocrites", "Oh ye of little faith". The seeker of wisdom has to realize that wisdom, while conveying information, also does things to the seeker of wisdom. It may give confidence, invite humility, demand reflection, shock, exasperate with paradox, tease.

Wisdom is "elitist"

But there is something else about at least some sorts of wisdom that is even more unpalatable. Not only is wisdom only understandable by the wise but it is not, as it were, meritocratic. Even if you make an effort there is no guarantee you will receive it. One of the better known Biblical parables is of the sower some of whose seed fell on different sorts of ground. Just before telling it, Christ is asked by his disciples why he speaks (to the crowds) only in parables. He replies that the disciples may know the mysteries of the kingdom of heaven, but not the people because they will not understand. Later in the Gospels, especially in *St John*, it is made clear that full knowledge is only for an elite. Indeed a whole part of the address at the Last Supper is made exclusively to the Apostles. In the early church non-members were not allowed into the second part of the Mass. The secrets were kept for those initiated. This sort of view that different layers of knowledge are suitable for different sorts of people is widespread in other wisdom literature. The secret is precious and must be guarded. It is a view not likely to endear itself to democratic America or Blairite modernizing Britain.

Expertise undermines wisdom

Some will dismiss this tension or war between wisdom and expertise. The two belong to different domains, they will say. Let's have modern technology for our motor cars and disease-destroying pharmaceuticals and wisdom for the lonely and dying. This may be achievable in some matters. In old age it is good to have the comforts of modern medicine, wealth and the independence that goes with it and also to have a respected place in society. But this accommodation may not be sustainable. Increasingly wisdom and expertise both lay claim to a common territory. For instance on welfare, marriage, poverty and crime the two have conducted a very noisy war. It also ignores another point. The problem is that expertise tends to drive out wisdom. Medical science encourages expectations it cannot satisfy, then when it needs wisdom, it finds that its narrow rationalism has driven out the morality and sensibility of wisdom. The new social sciences, much more unreliable than medical science, demand a monopoly for their statistics and theories in curing crime and poverty and bringing up children. They deride old fashioned insights about human nature and even more moral indignation. As T S Eliot wrote,

> *It is perhaps too much to expect of any man to possess specialized scientific power and wisdom [since] wisdom seems to be a commodity less and less available in educational institutions; for the methods and ideals...in modern education are not calculated to cultivate a disposition to wisdom.*[22]

Both the content and the form of wisdom demand a certain "disposition" and the content of modern lives, its aspirations and weaknesses and the forms of modern enquiry subvert this disposition. This is most obviously the case when wisdom is tied up, as it so often is, with religion. It was once the case, in the nineteenth century, that modern thought was anti-religious. Of twenty-first century persons it would be more accurate to say that they don't and perhaps can't understand religion. In either case, Maurice Cowling is right when he says that,

> *The Christian phase of European civilization may be over.*[23]

It is in this sense that we may rightly speak of wisdom being lost. Aristotle's *Ethics* is not lost and nor is The Bible. There are plenty of copies in second hand book shops. You can have the wisdom of Athens and God Almighty for the price of a hamburger. The texts of wisdom are more or less freely available, in both senses of that word. They may even be taught in some homes and schools. Yet the majority of the population has no appetite for them even in easily digestible dictionaries of quotations. There is no readiness to approach them with patience, reflection and humility, to let them work their magic. The war, declared on wisdom by a progressive "lettered arrogance" has been fought and is largely over. Wisdom interfered with those things that modern man thinks will give him pleasure. It offended his self-satisfied notion of himself. It required moral qualities of him that he no longer has or much cares about. So wisdom lost the war. The consequences of this loss for the Western civilization wisdom helped to build will not be long in coming.

CHAPTER 2

Falling in love, getting married and staying together

Lucy Sullivan

The young heroine of the 1990s film *How to Make an American Quilt* is undecided as to whether she should marry her rather inconsiderate boyfriend, and pays an extended visit to her mother and grandmother, hoping to draw on their wisdom as older women in making her decision. She meets her mother's circle of friends who might also be expected to be funds of wisdom, and questions them in turn about their marriages. Having made her survey, the girl decides that none of these older women had any useful advice to offer her. "So" she says to herself, "I will just have to work it out for myself."

"How ridiculous!" was my immediate thought, "and what a dangerous message. As if a young woman can possibly hope to invent for herself the meaning and rules of so age-old and difficult an institution as marriage." But on second thoughts I realized that, in the circumstances, this young, unassertive, sensitive girl had no obvious alternative. For there was only one lasting marriage among these vessels of sixties ideology; none had been happy with her marriage, nor had any a clear idea of what had gone wrong. The sexual and social revolution of the 1960s had sealed off access to traditional knowledge.

The Christian marriage promises define and advise

The shining beacon for the English-speaking world, the towering statement of what marriage is or should be – still there for the finding, although its advice is not quite at the level this young woman anticipated – must surely be the Form of the Solemnization of Matrimony in the *Book of Common Prayer*, put together by Cranmer in the mid-sixteenth century for the newly independent Church of England, and reprinted to this day. Marriage is a well-nigh universal human social institution whose variations in the way of polygamy and household composition do not disguise its central core of a male-female sexual relationship with domestic, economic, procreational and familial implications. It is undoubtedly innate, inescapable for humans as a species. The form of marriage prescribed in the *Book of Common Prayer* is the one which has shaped our culture until recently and still haunts us. We don't quite know how to manage without it.

Marriage, it says, "was ordained for the mutual society, help, and comfort that the one ought to have of the other, both in prosperity and adversity". These primary desiderata and obligations of marriage are reiterated, with greater force and finality, four times in the priest's interrogation of man and woman, and in their promises. The man must affirm that he will live together with the woman, "love her, comfort her, honour and keep her in sickness and in health; and forsaking all other, keep [himself] only unto her, so long as [they] both shall live", and the woman must affirm likewise.

And the man must, in his own voice, promise these things even more dramatically, taking the woman "to have and to hold from this day forward, for better for worse, for richer for poorer, to love and to cherish, till death us do part", and the woman likewise. These are very definite and specific statements about mutual obligation, daunting or comforting in proportion as one is inclined to view oneself as their provider or their recipient, but not beyond human powers of fulfilment. Taking for granted its role in the procreation and raising of children, has marriage ever been defined with higher aspirations?

The definitional promises of the marriage vows are virtually the same for the man and woman. The singling out of the woman to obey and serve has attracted much criticism in the wake of egalitarianism, while the one-sided obligation of the man to endow the woman with all his worldly goods (which perhaps goes some way to compensate the woman for her "service") has attracted less antipathy, and this could be considered remarkable. Curiously, only the man must promise to comfort, and he alone makes the thrilling and poetic declaration, "With my body I thee worship". Both these differences, it can be argued, show a wise recognition of sexual dimorphism.

Although this definition of marriage appears to consort so well with the ideals of romantic love (a second dominating influence in our culture), in fact the conception underpinning it is quite different. The understanding of romantic love is that it will come upon you and take hold of you as if from outside, without volition, and that only acquiescence or "spontaneity" on your part is required; that of the marriage ceremony is that love is something you must achieve for yourself, that you must promise and fulfil.

The emphasis on indissolubility in Christian marriage is its most unique characteristic; the imposition of exclusive sexual relations is more common. The requirements of mutual fidelity and permanence, in today's climate of opinion on matters sexual, are hard lines, but omit them and the high-minded content of marriage, and much of what we still aspire to in it, immediately begins to dissolve. To understand the implications of these special requirements of Christian marriage, we must look at it in the context of Christianity as a philosophical whole.

Pre-Christian marriage in the Western tradition

George Coughlan, in 1973, observed that,

> *In all societies and religions we know about there has been a close connection between religion and sex...Because sexual urges are so strong, all societies have felt the need to set limits to sexual behaviour.*[24]

Marriage in Ancient Greece was monogamous and divorce does not seem to have featured prominently. The position and freedom of women within marriage seem to have differed considerably in the various city states. As at most periods since, men seem to have felt that they had less control over their wives than they would like, and Socrates proposed the abolition of marriage, in favour of community-based sexual relations and child-rearing. This is a recurring zany dream of Western philosophy, but Socrates' vision was not quite the sexual paradise this suggests to the modern mind, for, he says,

> *It would be a sin either for mating or for anything else in an ideal society to take place without regulation.*[25]

He proposes that mating should take place only at special "festivals" during which lots will be drawn for partners; but the lots will be secretly organized by the Guardians (the ruling elite) so that reproduction is eugenic.

Aristotle was more practical, and offered an opinion which perhaps bears on our modern problem with wifely obedience:

> *The man rules in accordance with his worth and in those matters in which a man should rule, but the matters that befit a woman he hands over to her.*[26]

The husband should not attempt to rule in the wife's province, nor should the wife in the husband's, which latter sometimes occurs, he says, if the wife is an heiress. The wife's promise to obey, in the Church of England marriage ceremony, also reflects the universal division of labour between the sexes, and the fact that, while men are most unlikely to trespass on women's autonomy with regard to domestic management and children, women can and will interfere in men's affairs. The damaging potential of a wife's meddling in her husband's financial and professional affairs, at a time when women's formal work was largely domestic, is poignantly depicted by George Eliot in her characters Rosamund and Lydgate, in the novel *Middlemarch*.

Rather more is known of Roman marriage. Cicero described marriage as "the first bond of society".[27] A law attributed to the time of Romulus forbade the repudiation of wives other than on what have been the most generally accepted grounds for divorce, namely, infidelity and drunkenness. The Romans claimed that no one took advantage of their right to divorce in the five hundred years of the Republic, when civic virtue was at its height. However, divorce and serial monogamy became common under the Empire. The Emperor Justinian was thoroughly modern in arguing that,

> *If marriages are made by mutual affection, it is only right that when that mutual affection no longer exists, they should be dissoluble by mutual consent.*[28]

This ethic was, it should be remembered, one of a culture in increasing disarray, and is the foundation of present-day divorce law.

The third pre-Christian tradition of significance to Western civilization is, of course, the Jewish. Divorce was approved on the usual grounds of sexual misbehaviour, and was permitted, with penalties, on more trivial ones. Its availability was considered an important sanction for maintaining good behaviour in wives.

Marriage as sacred

Both the Greeks and the Jews mythologized the human drive to marry as something beyond mere copulation, by hypothesizing a single material origin of man and woman. The Greek version, which appears in Plato, that humans were originally a combination of male and female which split into two, so that each is continually seeking its other half, is perhaps the more egalitarian, but the Hebrew version is more moving. "The desire and pursuit of the whole is called love", says Plato detachedly, while the Bible, in *Genesis* 1, speaks poetically to deep human impulses, for which the taking of the rib is only a backdrop. God says,

18. It is not good that the man should be alone.

The creation of Eve is recounted, and then:

23. And Adam said, This is now bone of my bones, and flesh of my flesh...

Then follows a not entirely logical exposition which looks to the future institution of marriage:

24. Therefore shall a man leave his father and his mother, and shall cleave unto his wife: and they shall be one flesh.

The action of God, in creating man and woman in such a way as to create, also, marriage, gives marriage a sacred origin in the tradition which the Christian world inherited.

The fatuous modern "wisdom" that marriage is "just a piece of paper" denies any religious or "sacred" dimension to the ceremony; and indeed, with religion absent and marriage regarded as no more that an expression of transitory personal preference (in the tradition of Justinian), the statement is true enough. But if the promises of the ceremony are intended to be kept, then it is asking much of the individual to sustain them without the external support provided by religion, or alternatively by recognition of the embeddedness of marriage in the fabric of society.

The last two centuries, since the Enlightenment and the first major attack on Christianity's right to order the moral character of society, have seen a struggle between Christianity, represented by the churches, and its secular offspring, romantic love, for ideological control of marriage. Coleridge, at the initiation of the Romantic Movement, typifies the enlightened attacks on marriage with his declaration that,

Marriage…has no natural relation to love…it is a social contract.[29]

While the post-Enlightenment victory appeared briefly to go to love, it has since transpired that romantic love is unable to survive the death of its parent, Christian universal love, with any vestige of sacredness or spirituality. And so far, abstract "society" has proved to be no substitute for a concrete god, whose rules are explicit as "the word of God".

Karen Blixen, in her perceptive essay *On Modern Marriage*[30], written in 1923-4, observed that marriage in her day was now sanctified not by God but by "love". Love alone was seen as justifying marriage, she observed, and if it died, the marriage became "immoral". Blixen saw this as an unsafe transition, and argued that the personal rapture of love is inadequate to define marriage:

…the love relationship between a man and a woman [only] becomes a marriage when it is entered into in the recognition that the personal feelings of both partners – no matter how much they had based upon them – must be subordinate to, and serve, an idea that for both of them is higher than love itself…[31]

She compares the married partners and their marriage to a general and his army or a king and his people. The king/general is not everything to the people/army, or vice versa, but the integrity of the kingdom, and the winning of the war, are everything to them both. In effect, she puts society in the place of God in requiring permanence in marriage.

The revolt against marriage in the name of love was essentially against the strictures of fidelity and indissolubility. Is there any reason why we should keep such hard promises as Christian marriage entails? Social

24

structures and functions are integrally interdependent, and it may be that, as Blixen suggests, aspects of our society and our civilization which we value require the sacrifice of life-long, faithful marriage. Marriage is "normally" associated with religion and the desires of the gods or God, and the extra degree of conscience that Christianity brought to marriage was identical with that it brought to life in general, a subjective moral dimension as compared with the dogmatic requirements of religious custom and/or law, and herein may lie the importance of its special stringencies.

Christian marriage

Divorce, the prime target for marriage reform in the second half of the twentieth century, was, says Alvarez[32], more difficult under the Christian Church than it has been in any other culture. Divorce was rare and difficult to obtain in Western Christian nations from the tenth century, when the Popes assumed temporal power, until less than half a century ago. This, of course, raises the question of whether the indissolubility of Christian marriage was integral to the development of Western civilization.

The emphasis by the Christian Church on the indissolubility of the marriage bond is traceable to the words of Christ himself as reported in the Gospels. In *Matthew* 19, Jesus' response to questioning by the Pharisees, perhaps as a result of earlier statements he had made, revokes the laxer approach to divorce permitted by Mosaic Law:

> *3. The Pharisees also came unto him tempting him, and saying unto him, Is it lawful for a man to put away his wife for every cause?* [presumably *every cause allowable at the time*]

Jesus intends to say no to this, that there is only one ground for divorce, and he appeals to *Genesis*, to its declaration of God's creation of the first couple and the implications thereof. He says,

> *4. ...Have ye not read, that he which made them at the beginning made them male and female,*
> *5. And said, for this cause shall a man leave father and mother, and shall cleave to his wife; and they twain shall be one flesh.*

Thus, Jesus asserts, the making of husband and wife was the making of indissolubility, by God. So…

> 6. …*What therefore God hath joined together, let not man put asunder.*

He is then queried as to why, if his argument is correct, Moses permitted divorce. His reply is in the terms of his new teaching of universal love for one another, which will allow human beings to fulfil God's intentions more perfectly. He says,

> 8. …*Moses because of the hardness of your hearts suffered you to put away your wives: but from the beginning it was not so.*
> 9. *And I say unto you, Whosoever shall put away his wife, except it be for [her] fornication, and shall marry another, committeth adultery: and whoso marrieth her which is put away doth commit adultery.*

So there is the implacable logic – the joining of man and woman in the sexual act makes them one flesh; this is irrevocable and on this rests marriage. If either commits the sexual act with another, this is against God's word and can destroy the marriage, and the fornicator cannot begin again and become one flesh with someone else; nor can voluntarily divorced people. Is this psychologically and sociologically true, another example of Jesus' stunning gifts of insight into the tangled interactions of ethics and human nature?

For example, might the first sexual act in fact produce a kind of imprinting which cannot be repeated. If so it is squandered in premarital sex, just as the mother-baby capacity for bonding was squandered when babies were removed to a hospital nursery immediately after birth. Lorenz's observations suggest an effect of this kind in grey-lag geese, which are monogamous, but if one of a couple dies, the remaining partner fails to achieve a second monogamous relationship and becomes promiscuous. It may be that we are observing just such an effect in Western society in the close correlation of an increase in premarital sex and the phenomenal increase in divorce. And perhaps John Updike, the premier novelist of the age of divorce, recognized the innate monogamy of humans when he made one of his characters introspect that his life had been permanently "dislocated" by the break-up of his first marriage, even though he had sought divorce and had married again.

And sociologically, it is possible that the indissolubility of marriage for the first time gave the nuclear family the strength and stability to secede from the supportive structures of tribalism. We can observe in our own time how the increase in divorce has moved parents and children back into greater dependency on the extended family, and on the state in lieu of the tribe. Detribalisation is necessary both to the practice of Christian love (as defined in the Parable of the Good Samaritan) and to the functioning of Western civilization.

However this may be, the reference to men's hardness of heart before the time of Jesus' teaching of Christian love is, I think, at the crux of his position on the indissolubility of marriage, as appears in his words that follow. The disciples suggest that indissoluble marriage is rather too difficult an imposition, and that in these circumstances it might be better not to marry. But Jesus says, no, it is part and parcel of being able to receive the new Christian message of universal love, of loving thy neighbour as thyself, which he brings:

11. ...All [men] cannot receive this saying, save [they] to whom it is given.

And he goes on to direct harsh words of scorn at those who would avoid this divinely ordained human condition by not marrying:

12. For there are some eunuchs, which were so born from their mother's womb: and there are some eunuchs which were made eunuchs of men: and there be eunuchs which have made themselves eunuchs for the kingdom of heaven's sake.

Thus he rebukes his disciples for suggesting that they might find an easy way to holiness by avoiding the difficult task of indissoluble marriage. And he again stresses that those who receive his teaching must accept these conditions also:

12. He that is able to receive [it], let him receive [it].

This passage has sometimes been interpreted in quite the opposite direction, as linking celibacy with the kingdom of God, and indeed Paul appears to have been tempted to interpret it in this way. But the choice of the derogatory word "eunuch" makes this unlikely, and the passage seems, in context, far more likely to show Jesus characteristically reacting strongly to misinterpretation of his words. The interchange suggests that Jesus' direction that marriage should be life-long, indissoluble, was an integral part of his ethic of universal love, of its discipline: Only if you can discipline yourself to love your spouse, can you hope to fulfil the large command to love your "neighbour".

That is, "Charity begins at home". The sometime belief that domestic attachments detract from universal love and brotherhood (Plato, More, and some versions of Communism) is misplaced, and rather, one who fails to rise to the limitations and constraints imposed by love in the marriage relationship cannot be fit for the larger exercise of loving his neighbour. As Newman put it:

> How absurd it is when writers talk magnificently about loving the whole human race...That is not to love men, it is but to talk of love. The real love of men depends on practice...on cultivating an intimate friendship with those immediately about us.[33]

The idea that public policy should be "compassionate", to repair the effects of dereliction of duty, reflects a loss of understanding of what enduring and effective love entails.

Others have identified a failure of personal virtue with failure in marriage, for example,

> Divorce, the public brand of shameful life.[34]

And,

> It is not marriage that fails; it is people that fail. All that marriage does is to show people up.[35]

This view, though publicly unfashionable, is apparently privately resilient, for

> Couples seeking therapy are likely to bring intense emotion to the situation, to have invested considerable self-esteem in the success of the relationship, and to think badly of themselves for what may be seen as personal failure.[36]

Honour and obey

The imposition of a one-sided wifely submission has been, in recent years, a major target for criticism of the Christian concept of marriage as defined by the marriage vows. This obsession appears to derive from a mistaken interpretation of a Biblical injunction, this time of the words of the apostle Paul, in *Ephesians*. In fact, as in the marriage ceremony, the behaviour required of men and women, *vis* à *vis* one another, is the same, although the expression of this requirement (honour/love for men, and submission/reverence for women) is in different words.

In *Ephesians* 4, Paul warns his congregation against wrath and anger, and recommends love and forgiveness; moves on to warn against fornication, uncleanness and foolish talking; and continues:

22. Wives, submit yourselves unto your husbands, as unto the Lord.
23. For the husband is the head of the wife, even as Christ is head of the church: and he [meaning Christ, not the husband, surely] is the saviour of the body.
24. Therefore as the church is subject unto Christ, so let the wives be to their own husbands in everything.
25. Husbands, love your wives, even as Christ also loved the church, and gave himself for it:
26. That he might sanctify and cleanse it…
28. So ought men to love their wives as their own bodies…
29. For no man yet hated his own flesh; but nourisheth and cherisheth it, even as the Lord the church.

In its context, verse 22 seems to me to be about sexual relations in marriage, and not the marriage relationship in general. The "submit" is of the body, justified as the church is the body, and the bodies of man and woman are to be loved by the man as one. In I *Corinthians* 7, Paul has expressed the mistaken view that it is holier to be celibate than married. But now it is as if Paul is working hard, in a Greekish way, to revise his position on sex in marriage. Perhaps some husbands and wives had been influenced by his earlier position to refuse sexual relations to their spouses, and this was causing discord. Women are told not to turn away from sex as unspiritual and men to imbue it with love, not the carnality of the other.

After making this tangled web of associations amongst the human and the spiritual, Paul falls back on *Genesis* and "one flesh", and finally abandons the attempt at logic with the statement "This is a great mystery". The prefix to this passage is:

> *21. Give thanks submitting yourselves one to another in the fear of God.*

And his conclusion is:

> *33. Nevertheless let everyone of you in particular so love his wife as himself; and the wife see that she reverence her husband.*

So it would seem that undue interpretation has been given to this passage as regards unequal levels of autonomy for husband and wife in marriage – autonomy is not awarded to only one, but to neither. Today we prefer the words "love" and "honour" to "obey" or "submit", but in the context of the marriage vows the meaning is the same, as becomes clear if one applies them to one's relationship with the laws of one's country. One honours them, and this means much the same as obeying them. One loves one's country and voluntarily submits to its laws.

Coping with Christian marriage

How well did people fare during a millennium of indissoluble marriage which was meant to offer companionship, help, and comfort in prosperity and adversity, founded on love, honour and sexual fidelity? One might have thought that this difficult, but potentially rewarding, relationship would have brought forth a fund of deep wisdom in literature and philosophy. But few Western philosophers have been married, and writers have not been noted for committed marriages. Bertrand Russell's *History of Western Philosophy* has no entry on marriage after Thomas More's *Utopia* of 1518. The disparity in our literature between the paucity of attention given to the conduct of marriage and the almost surfeit given to romantic love, pre-marriage, in fact could scarcely be greater.

The wisdom of the past, as seen in proverb and epigram, has largely concentrated on telling the parties to marriage not to expect too much.

Perhaps this was because marriage was indissoluble – one had made one's bed and had to lie in it. Our proverbs mostly skate across the surface rather than cultivating the root stock of love on which marriages thrive. Proverbs and witticisms deploring marriage are common, but then, giving marriage a bad press could not, in the circumstances, increase the rate of exit.

Wedlock is a padlock
Early wed, early dead

Oh! How many torments lie in the small circle of a wedding ring, [37]

Marriage was also considered inevitable, although it has not been so universal in Christian countries as elsewhere, with only about 70 per cent typically marrying as compared with the more normal 100 per cent.

Marriage is destiny
Wives must be had, be they good or bad

Notwithstanding all that wit, or malice, or pride, or prudence will be able to suggest, men and women must at last pass their lives together. [38]

Even modern therapists admit its strange allure.

The creation of family…is not a sufficient explanation for the intensity with which adulthood is characterized by the search for an intimate partner. [39]

It is also admitted that the single state is just as bad in a different way.

It happens as with cages: the birds without despair to get in, and those within despair of getting out. [40]

One was never married, and that's his hell; another is, and that's his plague. [41]

Even the positive opinions on marriage are usually less enthusiastic and exuberant than one might expect, given our association of romantic love with marriage. Contentment is mostly its best fruit.

One year of joy, another of comfort, and all the rest of content

There is no such cosy combination as man and wife.[42]

One long conversation, chequered by disputes[43]

Charles Kingsley pointed out that even this is worthy of awe.

The life-long miracle, the self-begetting wonder, daily fresh[44]

Love, sex, companionship, and money are all significant elements in the establishment and continuance of a marriage, but are given different weights in different periods. All four feature in the marriage ceremony, although the last only as a disclaimer (for richer, for poorer). Nevertheless, money has been of considerable importance in English marriage, which is scarcely avoidable in a marriage culture of the nuclear family and household independence.

A poor man gets a poor marriage
A poor beauty finds more lovers than husbands
First thrive, then wive.
Who marries for love without money, hath merry nights and sorry days

The new emphasis put on love by the Romantics did not immediately dispose of the money question, and a prominent theme in Jane Austen's novels is the achievement of a wealthy marriage without abandoning the principles of love and good taste. The need to combine the two was recognized throughout the nineteenth century:

And all the young ladies said…a love match was the only thing for happiness, where the parties could anyway afford it.[45]

In the twentieth century, education and earning power became more important than inherited wealth. Opinion polls today show middle-class young men and women both setting value on equality of education and income in their partners.

The mid to late twentieth century concern with the quality of sex in marriage seems to be almost entirely absent in earlier periods, when the main worry was cuckoldry. Sex is merely acknowledged and assumed to be good. The marriage ceremony's "With my body I thee worship" is entirely positive. Alexander Pope, in the early eighteenth century, assumes mutual enthusiasm:

To church the parties went, At once with carnal and devout intent.[46]

However, Oliver Goldsmith, a little later, suggests less enthusiasm on the part of the woman:

He clasp's a goddess in his arms; And, though she felt his usage rough, Yet in a man 'twas well enough.[47]

Thus the twentieth century's belief in past repression of pleasure in sex may have been largely invented to serve the argument for extra-marital sex which assumed such importance at mid-century. Kenneth Barnes, in this context, warned young people that,

Sex is obviously important in marriage, but it is not of first importance. Friendship and companionship come first.[48]

The partnership of love and marriage is taken for granted in our early literature. "There as my heart is set, there will I wive," says the protagonist of Chaucer's *The Clerke's Tale*, and in Shakespeare's plays the aspiration is always to seal love with marriage. Nevertheless, in proverb and epigram, enthusiasm for love in the choice of marriage partner has been decidedly equivocal. By some it is positively disapproved.

It is unlucky to marry for love
Marriage is the tomb of love

Love, free as air, at sight of human ties, Spreads his light wings and in a moment flies.[49]

I rather suspect love is rather too violent a passion to make a good domestic sentiment.[50]

In the mid-twentieth century, Barnes also expressed caution.

> *Falling in love is a very untrustworthy experience...Yet it is shown*
> *on screen and stage as though it were the only experience that mattered,*
> *and as though the more rapidly it happened the more it could be*
> *depended upon).*[51]

But it is also unwise to marry without love.

> *'Tis love alone can make our fetters pleasant.*[52]

> *Where there's marriage without love, there will be love without*
> *marriage.*[53]

Marriage may create love.

> *Marry first and love will follow.*[54]

Satyajit Ray's 1950 film *The World of Apu* supports this possibility. His
young hero unwillingly marries a girl to rescue her from a disastrous
arranged betrothal, and is rewarded with a devoted mutual love. On
the other hand:

> *Marrying to increase love is like gaming to become rich; you only lose*
> *what little stock you had before.*[55]

There is considerable agreement on the simple do's and don'ts of
choice.

> *Marry your like.*

> *Like blood, like good, like age, make the happiest marriage.*[56]

But improving one's chances of happiness in marriage by a sensible
choice is not treated entirely encouragingly. Some advocate careful
choice, but others regard it as pointless.

> *The good or ill hap of a good or ill life, Is the good or ill choice of a good*
> *or ill wife.*

Marry in haste, repent at leisure.

But,

Marriage is a lottery.

It does not much signify whom one marries, as one is sure to find next morning that it is someone else.

If choice is unreliable and marriage inescapable, one might have expected a body of good advice on how to make the "prison" comfortable, but tolerance and compromise in dealing with the discomforts appear to be the sum of the advice from this quarter.

Keep thy eyes wide open before marriage, and half-shut afterwards.[57]

Marriage always demands the greatest understanding of the art of insincerity possible between two humans.[58]

The kindest and the happiest pair,
Will find occasion to forbear,
And something every day they live,
To pity, and, perhaps, forgive.[59]

Consider the following pair of proverbs,

A good husband makes a good wife.
A good wife makes a good husband.

These stress personal responsibility but without any specific guidelines. Thus the marriage promises to love, honour and comfort appear to be our clearest enduring instructions for the actual conduct of marriage.

The proverbs and epigrams of proven staying power, such as those quoted above, come from the top and the bottom of the intellectual spectrum – the yeoman and the academic philosopher, as it were. An intermediary level of opinion and advice on marriage has, I feel sure, always existed until recently – an ever changing oral tradition of advice on the details of married behaviour, and an equally changing published discourse at the sub-literary level of advice books and magazines. But the specificity of this advice to particular times and manners makes it vulnerable to changing fashions, while the more abstract pronouncements have remained in circulation. Views encountered from even the recent past can astonish the present, such as the tenet of only a few decades ago that a wife should change out of apron and day dress into fresh clothes to receive her husband when he returns home in the evening.

The overwhelming impression left by these surviving sayings is that marriage has nothing to do with gratification. The married state, they assert, is a difficult one, but inevitable, and is not really open to improvement. Stoicism is the only recourse. While they may have been psychologically stabilizing when marriage was indissoluble, they are likely to be harmful in an era when divorce is readily available. Through stressing the ills and difficulties of marriage, rather than its virtues and rewards, they may well increase its fragility.

Wriggling out of marriage

During the course of the twentieth century, marriage changed in its popular conception from a sacred and social institution to a private sexual relationship answerable only to the predilections of the individual partners. The modern attack on Christian marriage began with the simultaneous denial of its sacred nature and the substitution of what was considered a higher principle. Sexual infatuation (which I shall henceforth call "love", in inverted commas) was argued for as the moral basis of both sexual relations and marriage. Blixen, as we have seen, identified "love" as the supplanter of marriage, and analysed its unsuitability for this role. If one asked "modern educated people", she proposed,

> *What is it that changes a [sexual] relationship between a man and a woman from an immoral to a moral relationship?', then in 99 out of 100 cases the answer would be: "Love".*[60]

But, she points out,

> *Where love is the highest, indeed, the only law, a defection from it is an annulment of the whole relationship.*[61]

Giving moral priority to "love" permits it to challenge marriage without imputation of immorality. It is not wrong to break up a marriage, one's own or someone else's, for "love".

Guy de Maupassant wrote,

> It is love that is sacred...Marriage and love have nothing in common...We marry only once...but we may love twenty times...Marriage is law, and love is instinct. [62]

Noel Coward's 1920s revue sketch, *Shadow Play*, involving a separated couple, puts flesh on this development. *Surely if we're not comfortable together, the wisest thing is to separate*, says the man. *Everything was so lovely in the beginning*, responds the woman, longingly. *You can't expect what was lovely then to be lovely now*, the man replies, and only the resurrection of "love" could or should bring them together again. He sings

> If some forgotten lover's vow
> Could wake a memory in my heart again,
> Perhaps the joy that we knew would start again

Spontaneity is all.

The smart new ideas of one generation become the commonplace beliefs of the next. In the 1980s, this view was current in popular American culture. A sociological study of American soap operas,[63] found that when the hero or heroine fell in "love", it was taken for granted that prior relationships of marriage and parenthood should be sacrificed to it. "Love" had the status of a "holy fire", striking out of the unknown and demanding unquestioning obedience – and likely to strike many times.

When "love" in marriage is meant to survive spontaneously, it obviously cannot be assured, and so, according to the new realism, one cannot reasonably promise to continue to love. However, difficult requirements can bring out the best in people, and such "realism" sets low standards to which people readily fall. More's *Utopia* permitted divorce by mutual agreement on the grounds of discord, in theory, but permission of the Counsell was also needed, and its members would, he said, be

lothe to consent to it, because they know this to be the next [ie, fastest]
way to break love between man and wife, to be in easy hope of a new
marriage.[64]

In William Morris's version of Utopia, half a millennium later, an easy
compassion for failure obliterated such circumspection. Easy divorce
was to be the solution for "the unhappiness that comes of man and
woman, confusing the relations between natural passion, and sentiment,
and the friendship which, when things go well, softens the awakening
from passing illusions. Like Justinian, he decreed that,

> *...there need be no pretext of unity when the reality of it is gone: nor do*
> *we drive those who well know that they are incapable of it to profess an*
> *undying sentiment which they cannot really feel.*[65]

The moral primacy of love became the grounds for freeing sexual
relations from marriage when "love" recurred after marriage, but the
need for stability of marriage for the raising of children was initially
still recognized. Permanence, or at least semi-permanence, of marriage,
while permitting free "love", was advocated. Bertrand Russell, in 1929,
and Alex Comfort, in the early 1960s, hopefully proposed that marriage
could be maintained while "love" found sexual expression outside it.
Thus in *Marriage and Morals*, Russell argues that,

> *A marriage which begins with passionate love and leads to children*
> *who are desired and loved ought to produce so deep a tie that [the*
> *couple] feel something infinitely precious in their companionship...even*
> *if either or both feels sexual passion for someone else.*[66]

The problem, he says, has been jealousy, but though instinctive,

> *[Jealousy] can be controlled if it is recognized as bad, and not supposed*
> *to be the expression of a just moral indignation.*

Infidelity, he says, should not be grounds for divorce. This prospectus
did not work in Russell's own marriages, nor did it when tried on a
population scale in the 1970s. Jealousy, or the conviction that infidelity
denatured marriage, proved uncontrollable.

Alex Comfort's *Sex in Society*,[67] three decades after Russell, made much the same proposal, with the innovation that Comfort breaks the link between love and sex, which Russell maintained. His recommendation for extra-marital sex, without production of children, was well-timed for the arrival of the post-war baby boomers, who were reaching late adolescence and early maturity in a safe and stable society in which the security of marriage made no immediate appeal. According to Beatrice Faust, surveys in the 1960s still found that both men and women mostly thought sex should be for love, but by the 1970s sex could be for fun, without love or even "love".[68] Adulterous sex, supposedly without stigma, created strong pressures for easy divorce, and the case for maintaining the marriage while raising children was repudiated on the hypothesis that disputing parents caused children more harm than divorce. The solution of parents exercising restraint was not entertained.

When love was detached from sex, cohabitation in combination with sexual relations became marriage's only defining feature, and this new view of marriage became set in law – the new "no fault" divorce requires only that the spouses should have ceased sexual relations for a given, short, period. The terminology of "irretrievable breakdown of the marriage" is deceptive, as the couple may still cohabit, provided no copulation occurs. In addition to easy divorce, cohabiting sexual relationships were given equal treatment with marriage under the law, as *de facto* marriage. The churches bowed to these conditions, and thus Christian marriage as a social institution effectually disappeared.

Sex, now detached from both love and marriage, briefly became a superseding or primary good. The view of the sexual act as shameful in itself was attributed to Christianity as a central doctrine in this period, but in fact is an uncharacteristic development espoused by some eccentric Christian practitioners. Nevertheless, if sexual relations imply marriage, and marriage is to be lifelong, and sex outside marriage is fornication, logically this sets pretty tight limits on the number of sexual partners anyone can have in a lifetime, and some people see this as anti-sex. But there is no necessary derogatory implication as regards sex itself in Jesus' words or in those of the marriages promises. The metaphor of becoming "one flesh" from *Genesis*, repeated in *Matthew*, in *Ephesians*, and in the marriage ceremony, far from deploring it, sanctifies the sexual act as God-given.

Comfort saw Christian society as profoundly anti-sex, making the extraordinary statement that,

of all moral delinquencies sexual misdeeds are
[considered] the most serious.[69]

This despite the fact that neither adultery nor premarital sex have ever been criminal, unlike murder, theft, and treason! The Christian insistence that sex take place only within marriage, which was interpreted as primarily anti-sex, can equally well be interpreted as being primarily pro-marriage, since extra-marital sex destabilizes marriage. The claims that its intention was to subjugate women or to protect paternity are equally unfounded. The marriage promises are balanced between the sexes where they are not the same, and the Church never approved infidelity in husbands. If anything, its ruling was harder on male than on female sexuality.

The changes in the law and practice of love, sex and marriage in the latter half of the twentieth century have not produced greater happiness for the greatest number, although perhaps they reduced sexual tension in the young. Child abuse and youth suicide, desperate family crimes by divorced men and depression in women have all increased. The brave marriage "reforms" of the twentieth century have not resolved the impasse created by the undoubted urge to something like monogamy (marriage) and the co-existing on-going drive to attach to a mate ("love"), both of which are implanted in most human beings; and there probably is no personal solution since the second serves the first, but persists to undermine it.

The intense "search for a [lasting] intimate partner" did not disappear with free sex, which itself became something of a red herring in that search. Barnes, a Quaker, in a book of advice to young people, written a little after mid-century, expresses this need for love, which goes beyond both copulation and procreation, and can only be fulfilled by a relationship with permanency:

Human beings are much more than breeding animals, and when two people commit themselves to marriage they are not necessarily committing themselves to procreation. They are committing themselves to a joint search. [Search is] absolutely fundamental to human life...I see marriage as part of this universal activity. Human marriage – as distinct from animal mating – is not functional; it is not primarily a way of getting something done. It is not a way of settling down. It is a decision to share an adventure, to pool knowledge, resources, different sensitivities and temperaments in the search…, [and] not to be alone.[70]

With the guiding hand of both law and religion withdrawn, the human need for marriage became the property of the counselling professions, who secularised it as a "relationship", not different in kind from any other, and therefore still at the mercy of individual whim.

Relationships replace marriage

The popular canons of advice which have served to define marriage's constantly evolving lived characteristics have always been the work of the middling classes, and this tradition was robust so long as academic opinion was essentially confined to a small elite super-culture. Those who entered this culture eschewed popular wisdom and cleared their discourse of the traditions of speech and opinion they had grown up with, adopting the succession of supposedly rational post-Enlightenment views outlined above. With the expansion of tertiary education following World War II, the whole middle – and much of the middling classes were co-opted to this group, blanking out middling-class wisdom, and thereby stifling the ongoing generation of a vital theory of marriage to suit present circumstances.

But elitist theory does not provide everyday guidance for living. Counselling, an intellectually degenerate, macerated version of elements of the academic social sciences (which derive from the formerly elitist social theory) moved in to replace the old, informal, middling-class wisdom. In conformity with the new hegemony, the Marriage Guidance Council of Australia renamed itself "Relationships Australia", and similar revisions occurred in other English-speaking countries. From a scanning of the brochures produced and courses offered by two major counselling establishments in Australia which specialize in "relationships", one would think the institution of marriage no longer existed in our society. Definitions of the family do not include marriage. There are couples, and separation, but apparently not marriages. Marriage has no identity of its own.

The counselling offered to sustain "relationships" no longer, at the beginning of the twenty-first century, focuses on sex as it did in the 1970s when the "wisdom" was that

If a marriage goes on the rocks, the rocks are usually in the mattress.[71]

This has had its day. But nor is it about love. The positive aspects of relationships (love, comfort, help, companionship), whether married or other, have shrivelled to the avoidance of conflict, which is to be achieved by respecting "autonomy". Despite the fact that most couples seek counselling in order to stay together, counsellors are required, as professionals, to have no commitment to helping them to do so.

> *It is important for therapists…to remain open-minded…[as to] whether the relationship will improve or be broken up. Family therapists have at times been accused…of being in the business of keeping the institution of marriage going at all costs.*[72]

Another text notes the simplicity of couples who *react as if [marriage] were a true contract* which it can be wrong to break, when in fact marriage is *a concept not an entity.*[73] Counselling theory does not approve of assurances that effort put into a marriage will be reciprocated.

Counselling theory has reconstructed marriage as a relationship of autonomous individuals, and how marriage differs from other relationships, even in its obvious complications of cohabitation and child-rearing, is not touched upon, is unsaid. The possibility that marriage, as a lasting intimate relationship, might be damaged by autonomy is not admitted – rather, marriage must defer to autonomy and, if necessary, be let go. This template is, obviously, entirely inconsistent with the marriage vows, which declare and oblige, as a duty, the relinquishment of autonomy in certain respects; they demand recognition that there are certain things you must do, although they may offend against your autonomy.

If couples are, in fact, committed to marriage, there is nothing in the counselling agenda which tells them what they are committed to. Instead, it encourages them to renege on the difficult demands of the marriage promises. "Inappropriate" is the only judgmental epithet permitted in this interpersonal universe, but nevertheless practical benchmarks of what is appropriate are not provided. In fact, its identification still relies, in some vestigial way, on traditional concepts of right and wrong, although this is never acknowledged (for example, Corey on "Reality Therapy".[74]

Relationship counselling is, of course, a child of what Anderson calls

*[the] therapeutic sensibility...the touchy-feely Weltanschauung [which]
interprets all social and political life in terms of its relevance for
individual "growth", emotional well-being and gratification.*[75]

The advice books in its penumbra promote an ethical subjectivity of
astonishing self-centredness. Living well means feeling good, not doing
good;[76] all choices are right;[77] feeling loved (via the power of positive
thinking) is indistinguishable from being loved, and forget about
loving;[78] every trouble is an illusion of personal insecurity and can be
solved by not feeling insecure.[79] The emphasis in relationships
counselling is on what one can get out of the relationship, while that of
the marriage vows is on what one must give.

Attempting to engage with counselling on "relationships" is like
entering a white-out, an intellectual one, in which one must keep walking
but without any external signs to guide or objective sense of direction.
Plato's and Russell's proposals, absurd as they are, do not induce this
sense of mental fog, for they propose specific courses of action in the
real world. Relationship counselling only tells you to examine your
own feelings and to manipulate the feelings of others so as to placate
your own. You may keep yourself upright, but you still don't know
where you are, or where or if there is a goal, whether the safety of a hut
or the glory of a mountain peak.

Even the cruel proverbs and quotations of our recent forbears come
closer to providing clarity of purpose, if an unwelcome one. Counselling
gives no clues as to how to achieve the intimacy which, it is
acknowledged, is dearly sought. There is nothing here to match the
specificity of the marriage promises of love, honour, comfort, in sickness
and in health, for richer, for poorer, and certainly no suggestion that
compassion is a virtue in domestic, as well as in public, life.

Happy marriages

The elevation of love and sex above marriage produced some daunting
and ambitious prognostications for love in marriage – attempts to
express in Western philosophical language the aspirations conveyed
simply as an image in the Biblical phrase "one flesh".

The essence of a good marriage is respect for each other's personality combined with that deep intimacy, physical, mental, and spiritual, which makes love between man and woman the most fructifying of all human experiences.[80]

Coughlan, grappling with the ascendancy of sex, suggested that,

Ideally, and at its highest and best, the union of bodies expresses a union of minds and a strong feeling of "love" in its widest sense.[81]

Now that the testing of the hypotheses that love and sex are substitutes for, indeed are higher than marriage, has brought society to its knees, it appears that at the stout middling level, people are finding the humility to accept just simple companionship, with the addition of a few ritual frills like white wedding gowns and Valentine's Day flowers, as a very great good. Four couples of various ages who were asked by the *Hawkesbury Independent,* on St Valentine's Day 2002, to "share their secrets for good relationships" offered "friendship", "tolerance and common sense", "shared hobbies and fine meals" and our old familiar "give and take". Infidelity or "cheating" is definitely out. Far from jealousy being eradicated, there is a growing market in private investigation to confirm (or not) suspicions. Young people talk of "trust", which also implies being trustworthy.

Cultural fashions and practices can generate or destroy wisdom, and opinionated intellectualism is the worst destroyer. The generation of wisdom depends upon something like the processes of common law, a slow accretion of knowledge of what works, with only minor variations ventured at any one time to accommodate changes in circumstances. Wisdom is not systematic. It provides a random set of searchlight illuminations of restricted but significant aspects of long-founded practices; and the getting of wisdom is one's personal selection from among them. This may not provide a coherent approach to life's tasks, but it offers a set of guideposts, together with the sense of mental and emotional security which comes from knowing that others have passed the same way. The girl in *How to Make an American Quilt* hoped to glean this sort of security from her mother's generation, but found it sadly missing.

The marriage ceremony goes beyond wisdom; it is programmatic. We need to be clear about what the programme of marriage is, and we need wisdom to live out that programme. In a lifetime of books, plays, films and talk, I have encountered only six unforgettable guideposts, or perhaps I should say lamp posts, or shafts of illumination:

The mother of the romantic young sisters who, in the Russian film version of the opera of Pushkin's *Eugene Onegin*, expressed the acceptance she had learned for her arranged marriage to an older man in the gentle words, *Sweet habit takes the place of passion.*

The farmer in Hardy's *Far from the Madding Crowd*, looking forward to marriage as the simple comfort of unquestioned companionship, who expressed his deep longing with the image of husband and wife sitting by the fireside, and when either looks up, *There I'll be* and *There you'll be.*

Tolstoy's comment that Anna Karenina's deep problems arose because she had not the trust in Vronsky's affection, without marriage, to move from the role of mistress or lover to that of wife (and the revelation that they might be different).

The advice on marriage given by an old woman servant in Lawrence's *Lady Chatterley's Lover*, not to seek justice in every quarrel – she and her husband each gave in if the other cared more passionately about the issue, whether right or not.

In one of Anthony Powell's *Dance to the Music of Time* novels, the narrator's sense of the unsayableness of what makes a marriage, and his unwillingness to give an assessment of his own marriage, not good, not bad, other than, *It works.*

In retrospect, I can see that in these choices I was providing grounds, like the proverbs, for not expecting marriage to provide, permanently, the exaltation of romantic love, and was putting in its place the stoicism necessary for the long haul. The myth of Pandora's Box promises hope to help us through the stings and vicissitudes of living, and my sixth guidepost provides this counterpoint: the prospect of peace from the long battle to keep domestic life decent, offered by an elderly gentleman (actually in the prime of life in his sixties), encountered just once and briefly, who said of his marriage, with children grown up and gone, *These are the golden years.*

The concentration of literary attention on getting mated began at about the time of Shakespeare, when marriage changed from being predominantly determined by social and economic forces and circumstances to being predominantly a matter of personal choice, a task which the young must, to a considerable degree, perform for themselves, and at which they might fail. As noted above, the tremendous cultural energy that goes into the business of getting mated could scarcely be in greater contrast with the paucity directed to support the task of staying married. The recent freeing up of sexual encounters has not, apparently, made the former task any easier and, if anything, the cultural frenzy has increased as, with high levels of divorce, finding a mate has become a task for all ages.

Now that remaining within marriage has become a personal task and problem also, perhaps the arts will begin to take up marriage as a subject of immanent concern. Their orientation in the last half century has been primarily towards undermining marriage in the interests of "love" and promiscuous sexuality; one hopes that they will be able to reorientate to assist in the preservation of a relationship and institution we cannot do without.

CHAPTER 3

Doing one's work

Jon Davies

Wisdom is addressed to the wise

In a written tradition going back over two thousand years, the "Sages" of Israel and their "Wisdom" books comprise a source of commentary on (amongst other things) work and the related matters of ownership, poverty, prudence, liberality, age, and sex. The written record derives from a much older oral tradition. In the tradition, "Wisdom" in both Hebrew and Greek is in the feminine gender; and is seen as the personified expression of God. (A Bibliographical Note on Wisdom literature is to be found at the end of this chapter. Biblical references are, with one exception, to the Authorised King James Version, with the initial number the Chapter number, followed by the number of the verse(s).)

Present day "equivalents" such as "Working Time Directives" or "Personal Development Plans" are of a different order to the Wisdom literature. They are primarily work-place or occupationally-specific, as if what a person does there can be somehow separate from what he or she is, or does in life in general. They are self-promotional, seeing the self as something to be consciously (cynically even) manipulated in order to manipulate others. They are primarily concerned with career and money and the benefits which may accrue to the self-manipulating individual rather than to the moral universe occupied by such an individual or, indeed, to the moral universe of society: and they are (oddly perhaps) replete with contingent insurances against any career-damaging steadfastness or character, such as the "Dare to be a Daniel" self-venturing of earlier days.

Such "Daniel" individualism cannot be subsumed into the world of "mission statements" and "personal plans" which, amongst other things, assume that all, no matter how mediocre, must have prizes and that "standing out" of the crowd is tantamount to being left out of it. "Personal transferable skills" are good, "character", where that implies idiosyncrasy, is bad. Psychometric testing and the psychology of self-advertisement invoke a world occupied by people whose "career guidance" is in the hands of "human relations managers", a world best summed up in David Riesman's 1951 *The Lonely Crowd*, a perceptive and prescient piece of writing whose title alone contains an analysis.

The Wisdom books such as the *Book of Ben Sira* (hereafter *Ecclesiasticus*) or *Pirke Aboth* (Sayings of the Fathers) are moral and didactic discourses, aimed at passing on the wisdom of the ages. *Pirke Aboth*, incorporated in the Mishnah, is perhaps the book most widely read by Jews over many centuries. In the main, the "Wisdom" tradition consists of "words to the wise", advice that is offered in the expectation that its hearers will have the sense to take note. Wisdom is not meant for fools. The words are more often warnings rather than straightforward prescriptions or proscriptions: for example, the comment that money can corrupt does not mean that it always will. The wisdom is often expressed in proverbs and fables, sometimes in almost wilful conundrums:

> If I am not for myself, who is for me? And when I am for myself, what am I? And if not now, when? [82]

Much fun could be had trying to relate *that* to Adam Smith's proverbial comment on the motivations and mechanisms of exchange between the butcher, the brewer and the baker and the would-be recipient of their services. Wisdom statements *can* be peremptory, and in the case of the Book of Job are powerfully admonitory and threatening – see below.

Wisdom as the foundation of Non-conformist Christian work culture

The "Wisdom" books of the Bible are a major source of the work-wisdom of our culture, well read over many centuries and propagated in churches, chapels and Sunday Schools. In many a red-brick Horeb,

Hebron, Bethesda, Soar or Bethel, assembled Christians pored over the ancient Jewish texts. As a major component of the Bible, they were the relevant texts for hard working men and women. The strength of this Wisdom tradition will be illustrated by reference to the lives of the "respectable working class", especially Welsh Chapel life. There is an ample literature on this subject, some of which is referred to in the Bibliographical Note at the end of this essay. It should be noted that the men and women who carried this culture were as "bourgeois" as they come, differing only from their middle class fellows in that they engaged in manual work. In a different mode, George and Weedon Grossmith's *The Diary of a Nobody* gives us, in Lupin Pooter, the first Yuppie, illustrative of the beginnings of the general breakdown of the nexus of family life, work and inter-generational relationships. Lupin is the Wisdom, working class and "bourgeois" tradition transgressed, the "Lonely Crowd" in the making.

The Sages can be cheerful – or even, apparently, irresponsible!

> *Then I commended mirth, because a man hath no better thing under the sun, than to eat, and to drink, and to be merry: for that shall abide with him of his labour the days of his life, which God giveth him under the sun.*[83]

While the Lupin Pooters of this world might eagerly welcome, by misinterpreting, the above comments of the author of *Ecclesiastes*, it may to some of us seem odd to begin an essay on work with a dismissal of it as a waste of time. A similar dismissal is to be found in *Matthew* 6, 26 and *Luke* 12, 27, where we are invited to follow the example of birds and lilies, neither toiling nor spinning. Yet, in an essay which may be rather "heavy", a presentation of a cheerful or benign view of the human condition may help to provide a corrective to the rather bleaker (if more realistic!) comments which follow, especially those taken from the bleakest of all "Wisdom" writing, the *Book of Job*.

> *Where were you when I founded the earth?*
> *Has the rain a father?*
> *Or who conceived the dewdrops?*
> *From whose womb emerged the ice?*
> *And the hoar-frost of heaven, who begot it?*[84]

Job's grim version of the trite saying that "*the world doesn't owe you a living*" would probably not figure in any modern manual of career guidance. Yet the wisdom of the Sages is impossible to understand, and its pleasures hard to perceive, without understanding its view that life, *where possible at all, is an accomplishment,* not a given; and that it is highly precarious. While for many of the Sages, Order was immanent in Creation, Job reminds us that human beings are well advised to consider that the Creator may well be totally indifferent to their particular existence. There is little in the Wisdom texts of the Sages which is as bleak as the *Book of Job*: yet in the precariousness of the human condition lies the proper comprehension of the significance of work and of the understanding that the Sages had of it.

Work exists for a purpose broader than the contribution it may make to the "happiness" or otherwise of the individual worker. Throughout these ancient texts, work, whether of deity or human, is seen as the basic method whereby Chaos is kept at bay – though never vanquished – and the means whereby individual humans can attain some degree of independence and life-enhancement. "Happy humans, happy workers" are well thought of: but they do not work necessarily and only to be happy. Work, miserable work even, is unavoidable if "society", the efforts at survival of men and women, is to even begin to measure up to the task of living with and in some sense managing Chaos and Disorder.

The purpose of work is to keep Chaos at bay

This truism would not bear repeating if we (and presumably Job) were not surrounded by millions of people who seem able to ignore it, spending their lives (and everyone else's substance) in a perpetual Gap Year. Anthony Crosland famously claimed that "*the problem of production has been solved*". In the apparent effortlessness and irreversibility of our economic progress and plenitude lies the source of this attitude. The Sages would regard Anthony Crosland's claim as blasphemous, stupid and dangerous. The only other claim which is as stupid and blasphemous and dangerous is the belief that we no longer need to bother about the procreation and nurturance of children. They too, of course, are both joy and an addition to the work-force: Work and Multiply, say the Sages, otherwise there will be no human society. The

Decalogue reflects this understanding, being primarily concerned with God, Work and Children.

In the Job verses quoted above, we should note that God claims power and pre-eminence because of His work: He is the first worker by hand *and* by brain, the exemplar of the relationship between work and proprietorial rights. The universe is His because he made it. Isaiah has a somewhat more benign deity promising righteous people "the land for ever, the branch of my planting, the work of my hands".[85] Human beings *are* God's work. Shemaiah said:

> *Love work and hate mastery: and make not thyself known to the government.*[86]

As career guidance this doesn't get you very far – but then career guidance, playing with slots for slotees, assumes the existence of a world of predictable and manipulable "invitations to work" unknown to (or denied by) the writers of earlier days. For Shemaiah and the Sages "career guidance" was the inculcation of a set of attitudes, not the filling out of job applications: and the aim of instruction was to locate work in a sense of human purpose and precariousness, not to get too bothered about qualifications, salary ranges, personal transferable skills or fringe benefits.

Work as part of the human condition

Shemaiah/Shamai/Sameas is a difficult figure to locate in history, and his comments are somewhat inscrutable. Perhaps the important thing to notice at the outset is the association he makes between these three precepts: work, mastery, control (by which he means the relationship between a worker and the state).

Maimonides[87] invites us to think of Shemaiah as saying that there are three, related, sources of injury to a man's faith, ie to the meaning, prosperity or virtue of his life. One, the neglect of work leads to dishonesty. Two, seeking or acquiring high rank exposes a man to the temptations of power. Three, to be intimate with rulers can encourage conceit or undue ambition: generally governments will "take notice" of a man only to use him for its own purposes. Governments are a vested interest, not the fount of disinterested altruism. You may work for them on that basis, but beware! Shemaiah, probably writing over two thousand years ago, spoke directly to my paternal grandfather who, as a boy, went to work in the coal mines of Glamorgan, and who was by age 29 too ill to work in the coal industry. He bought a horse and cart (later a van) and, getting up in the dark of the early morning, he travelled the valleys of South Wales selling soap, paraffin and other household goods. I never heard him grumble, though he did express regret about the fact that, as a boy, he had had to leave school early as the family needed his wages – but that was a regret, not a complaint:

> *Whatsoever thy hand findeth to do, do it with thy might.*[88]

He went to Chapel – except when he fell out with the Elders – and on the birth of his first son "took the pledge", having been something of a roisterer when young. He was a supporter of Plaid Cymru, a writer of Welsh poetry, and a reader of the Bible in Welsh. He worked, quite explicitly, so that his sons never had to work in the mine, although he developed doubts about what they did eventually do, especially when his eldest son, my father, left and divorced his wife, my mother. That was something beyond what he thought men should do. He understood that

> *The poor man toileth for the needs of his house, and if he rest he becometh needy.*[89]

not that he would have *ever* tolerated a description of himself as "poor".

Individual responsibility and work

Throughout *The Sabbath Day*, a BBC film about men and women such as my grandfather, there is the awareness that while there are indeed "structural" or impersonal sources of misfortune, the best and immediately relevant response is an individual one. The same picture emerges from the work by Norman Dennis *Coal is Our Life* and other studies of and novels about respectable working class life. These late nineteenth/early twentieth century workers correctly saw in texts such as the story of *Exodus* or the *Book of Proverbs* guidance which offered not simply an escape *from* slavery but also the escape *into* a personal responsibility for their own fate. My grandfather was perfectly aware of the power of "Pharaoh" (seen by him as English and as coal-owner), and perfectly aware that "impersonal forces" ruled in the world. He also knew, though, that in his own hands lay much the of obligation to work his way out of the circumstances these forces and Pharaohs created. There was no whinge in the analysis.

For the men in particular this meant dedication to hard work in a hostile market place, and the avoidance of intemperance or licentiousness in matters of sex and alcohol. The sluggard who was advised in *Proverbs* 6, 11 to consider the ways of the ant was warned that to ignore her example was to invite poverty *"as one that travelleth...an armed man"*. By this, the author(s) of *Proverbs* meant that a descent into poverty and dependency, once made, would or could be inescapable, partly because poverty (lived out as sloth and lying in bed) had, and has, its attractions and temptations.

Long before the 1834 Poor Law Report and Poor Law Amendment Act, the Sages knew that the demoralization implicit in poverty or dependency could create an underclass culture antithetical to self-reliance and positive social activity. As will be seen below, they were not at all against charitable giving to the poor, but always in the context of a concern for its dangers:

> *No return of kindness cometh to him that giveth satisfaction to the ungodly, nor hath he done any act of benevolence.*[90]

The Sages also knew that the very existence of a permanent or near-permanent underclass would be damaging to the broader society as well as to the underclass itself:

> *A naughty person, a wicked man, walketh with a froward mouth...Frowardness is in his heart, he deviseth mischief continually; he soweth discord.*[91]

Every working class community (and every Sage) knew from experience that lax leisure and sexual habits led to, or were, associated with lax work habits and an undermining of the essential work-place patterns of reliability, punctuality and effort within which individual accomplishment would or could be successful. For this reason, attitudes to work were constructed within a general ethic of moral-cultural and communal self-help and related institutions: orchestras and choirs of varying degrees of complexity, sports facilities and activities, clubs aimed at keeping working people out of pubs and instead in tune with drama, poetry reading and recitation. Trade unions, debating clubs, chapels and Sunday Schools were (then) part of this self-regulating culture, dependent on success at work for their continued vitality; indeed, many of these activities such as music making and sports were work-place related. They created friendship networks, putting pleasure and purpose into work, not perhaps as its fundamental purpose, but providing the "sign language" which made possible the mutual trust and mutual respect necessary for the informal organization of the work-place and the functioning of civil society.

They knew, as did R Dosa b Harchinas, that

Morning sleep, and midday wine, and children's talk, and sitting in the meeting houses of the vulgar, drive a man out of the world.[92]

For people like my grandfather in such a society, or more properly engaged in creating such a society, the advice about work and its relationships contained in *Proverbs* 27-28-29, advice which they knew from pulpit and Sunday School, made sound practical sense. Greedy people cause dissension; constructive criticism will, in the end, be more mutually beneficial than flattery; honesty in dealings is the best policy; concern for the poor, the powerless, the needy will lead to justice, while ignoring the matter will not; corrupters of honest men will bring about their own fall; the company of good men with each other reinforces virtue; people who deal dishonestly with family members are worse than thieves; better poor than dishonest; keep good care of your capital goods and equipment, as such things do not last for ever; no two men are the same; don't trust a weak man in times of trouble; lack of self-control brings destruction; sloth begets more sloth; don't bandy words with a fool , lest you become one; do not boast about your accomplishments, as they may not last; work for and take a fair share and no more.

Work and women

For women too, in pre-Roman Israel and twentieth century Glamorgan, the Sages provided advice. Put your back into your work, and show how well you can work; be busy, with wool and linen, getting up before dark to prepare the day for the household; look for and acquire property, earn income from it, make your own household domestic linen and bedding; be considerate to the poor and to servants; preside over the household; and in doing all these things you will earn the confidence and love of your husband and of your children, and will earn the respect and esteem of the community.[93] Take care with beauty,

As a jewel of gold in a swine's snout so is a fair woman which is without discretion.[94]

Many a "model" strutting her ephemeral stuff in the idiot columns of glossy magazines might benefit from this advice.

The nature of the participation in work and communal life was clearly understood by the Sages to vary with age – there was a life course. Details varied, but by about twenty a man was expected to have completed his education and training, to be married and to move into work. In this phase men assume moral responsibility. Between twenty and seventy this training and preparation are brought to personal, familial and communal fruition. It is during those years that his "real work" is done. He is, for example, at "full strength" at 30, capable of discernment at 40, of giving counsel at 50, of getting old at 60, grey hairs at 70. By 80, work is becoming full of sorrow; and he enters the third period, of decline, senility and death.[95] This was all perfectly natural, if somewhat unfortunate.

A variety of consequences flowed from this, including what we would call age "discrimination".

The glory of young men is their strength; and the beauty of old men is the hoary head.[96]

Discrimination is a general virtue: and in the work place, on grounds of age, the Sages felt that it made a lot of sense. To be indiscriminate is silly – a truism, but at the time of writing we read of proposed legislation making it illegal to discriminate on grounds of age (and sex and religion): so that the Corps of Commissioners may have to take on 16-year-old females.[97]

The physical strength of the young, and their capacity for manual labour was valued by the Sages and by men who worked down mines or on the roads and other construction sites. Ford Madox Brown's 1865 painting *Work* illustrates the nature of the life cycle and functional division of labour. The picture shows a group of navvies digging a trench in London, led by the central figure of the lithe strong young man, dominating the work of his older, stouter comrades, one swigging a pint of beer – a healthy beverage. The young man is the older men's past, they in turn being his future. Older, non-manual men – the workers by brain – and women look on or are busy in their own way. In the background a much wealthier couple on horseback approach the "hole in the road". The painting is "busy", with complications added in by the artist in response to a potential buyer's desire that it should contain material of moral and religious significance. The painting was regarded by Ford Madox Brown as illustrating (amongst other things) the physical strength required for certain tasks, and the physical changes which occur in the course of manual work, as well as the other co-incidental differences that age and the division of labour were making in an increasingly wealthy society.[98] Ford Madox Brown of course was an active participant in F D Maurice's Working Men's College, another voluntary respectable cultural institution, for attendance at which working class men would take care to wear their "Burton" suits and ties:

> *Comely is study (of Torah) with worldly occupation, for toil in both makes sin forgotten.*[99]

The Sages comment that health is important for work: and that in part a concern for health in youth could provide some way of dealing with the inevitable infirmities of old age. This was well understood in South Wales, which along with many working class communities had insurance-based health and funeral care and income maintenance facilities long before compulsory State-derived provision.

Mutual dependence of old and young

Then, as now, the viability of such provision depended on youthful health and work, and on the availability of new workers, ie babies. In Millais' *Christ in the House of His Parents* (1850), Jesus is shown in his father's workshop, where men (and women) are shown working on building a door in what is clearly the work-place of a skilled carpenter, and therefore by the standards of the time and by those of today a relatively well-paid man. (Some kind of snobbery sees this trade as making Jesus "poor", thereby indicating how little such commentators know about working class work: Joseph couldn't get into the inn because there was no room, not because he was poor: few skilled men are.) The painting, though, emphasizes the role of the older people in training the young; and the Sages and the Wisdom literature are full of references to this mutuality.

It has to be said that in this picture the young Jesus does not look too happy. While *Proverbs* 17, 6 has *"the glory of children are their fathers"*, perhaps at this point in his life Jesus would have agreed with Lupin Pooter that *"an old and a young horse can't pull together in the same cart"*.[100]

The new labour force had to be skilled: and for the children at the beginning of their lives, working class communities shared with the Sages an extraordinary veneration for schooling and learning. In South Wales, voluntary and other school facilities, and indeed the basis of what became University colleges, ensured that to a greater or lesser extent young people could share in, and so contribute to the stability and prosperity of the world they worked to make. In a way which would have pleased (perhaps!) the Sages, to whom study of the Torah was the serious point of maturity, the Welsh changed in three generations from being a nation of manual workers to a nation of professional teachers and scholars. They lost, however, the ability to play rugby and to sing.

Independence through work

Shamaiah, who appeared earlier, concluded his thought with *"make not thyself known to the government"*. There is a wealth of wisdom in this comment, which would take pages to disentangle. Amongst other things, it calls attention to the desirability of being independent:

Better the life of the poor under a shelter of logs than sumptuous fare in the house of strangers.[101]

And for many of the workers in mines and fields, worshipping in

Hebron, Soar, Bethany and Horeb, Sion and Bethesda, oppressed in ways in which we do not now see, the answer lay in yet another of the precepts of the Sages and of the culture which they created – emigration, the greatest and most successful job and wealth creation project of all time, in which a variety of Pharoahs were escaped in order to free the labour of millions of men and women, to create free and hard-working societies all over the world.

In conclusion:

Give not thy soul to sorrow
And let not thyself become unsteadied with care
Heart-joy is life for a man
And human gladness prolongeth days.[102]

There is nothing miserable about even the most minatory prescriptions of the Wisdom literature: they are genuinely joyous – and genuinely wise.

Bibliographical Note

The output of the Sages and the Wisdom Tradition are not synonymous, though in this short essay I have tended to treat them as such. Most of the "writing" can be located in the centuries of 300 BCE to 300CE.

Much of the Wisdom literature can be found in the Bible. This can be supplemented by R H Charles *The Apocrypha* and *Pseudepigrapha of the Old Testament* in English (OUP, 1968). In sum, Wisdom literature "proper" consists of the Book of Sirach, referred to in this essay as *Ecclesiasticus*; the *Book of Job*; a number of the *Psalms*; *Proverbs*; *Ecclesiastes*; *The Wisdom of Solomon. The Sages*, by E E Urbach (Hebrew University Press, 1975) and *Pirke Aboth: The Sayings of the Fathers* (trans. R Travers Herford, Schocken Books, NY, 1962) complete the necessary reading. *The Book of Legends, Legends from the Talmud and Midrash*, edited by Bialik and Ravnitzky, Schocken Books, NY, 1992 is instructive fun to dip into. David Wolfers *Deep Things out of Darkness: the Book of Job* (Eerdmans Publishing Co., Michigan, USA, 1995) is a fine book.

Studies of English "class" cultures are summarized in Josephine

Klein's *Samples from English Culture* (RKP 1965) and presented, in a different way, in Richard Hoggart's *Uses of Literacy* (Chatto and Windus, 1957). Miners' lives are now almost part of semi-romantic folk-lore, as in various pastiches of *How Green Was my Valley* or in DH Lawrence's *Sons and Lovers*, where they are depicted as repressed and bigoted, or, more recently, the film *Billy Elliott*. Norman Dennis' *Coal is Our Life* (Tavistock, 1969) is the best single account of miners, while *Glowyr De Cymru* (The Miners of Wales) by RP Arnott (Allen and Unwin, 1967) should be read along with a viewing of *Remember The Sabbath Day*, a 1989 BBC1/BBC Wales, Everyman documentary, about Welsh Chapel culture, which is brilliant. A J Cronin's *The Citadel* (Vista books, 1996) gave another "twist" to the story.

The Diary of a Nobody, by George and Weedon Grossmith, (Elm Tree Books, London 1984), is the anti-Wisdom book, though wisdom does seem to peep in at the end. The "Diary" appeared originally in Punch in the 1890s. Davis Riesman's *The Lonely Crowd* was published in 1951 by Yale University Press.

See also J M Golby *Culture and Society in Britain 1850-1890*, a Source Book of Contemporary Writings (OUP with the OU, 1988), pp 112-118 on Ford Madox Brown's *Work*.

CHAPTER 4

Making and keeping friends

Digby Anderson

Only the friendship of those who are good, and similar in their goodness, is perfect. For these people each alike wish good for the other qua *good…and it is those who desire the good of their friends for the friends' sake that are most truly friends because each loves the other for what he is.*[103]

The soul of Jonathan was knit with the soul of David, and Jonathan loved David as his own soul.[104]

A father writes to *The Times (London): My son, 10, finds it hard to make friends.* A children's charity expert "parenting adviser" replies that:

One should interfere as little as possible but that if the lack of friends is upsetting the son, the father should "work on this" as it might damage the son'" self-esteem". He should "role play the skills involved in approaching friends" such as eye contact and smiling.[105]

London's evening paper, *The Standard* reporting on the party for Alexandra Shulman's 10 years as editor of Vogue explained that it would be *for 350 of her closest friends.* Miss Shulman agreed that she had *lots of friends* and pointed out, *I just love them.*[106]

Wisdom warns against seeking happiness directly

I recently watched the English seeking happiness with their friends in a small southern town. The town has a main street that leads down to the beach and the sea. The beach was full of holiday-makers, families and groups of friends playing games, bathing, chatting, sleeping, all intent on pleasure of one sort or another. The main street is full of cafes, restaurants, bars and shops, again thronged with people queuing to buy the things which make them happy.

Also in the main street is a second-hand book shop. On the shelves labelled "Religion and Philosophy", subjects which are also, to an extent, about happiness, are several Bibles and a copy of Aristotle's *Ethics*. It is often claimed that these two, and several other of the titles around them – there was a selected Cicero there – are the most valuable sources of wisdom in the world. In an interesting phrase, it is sometimes said that they contain "the secrets" of true and long-lasting happiness. The people outside on the beach and in the bars and shops obviously think otherwise. If the books contain secrets it is largely in the sense that their contents are ignored. The books have been there for some months now and their price reflects the worth society accords them; both the revelation of Almighty God and the wisdom of classical Greece can be yours or anyone's for less than the price of a small hamburger.

Interestingly, these two books can claim also to contain the secrets of friendship, or of wisdom about friendship. And, though friendship, like happiness, is said to be much sought in modern society, no-one is much interested in what Aristotle or the Old Testament have to say about it.

It is easy to see why the fun-loving population ignores the wisdom on happiness and friendship. Some little effort is involved in learning from them and effort is not popular. But also their wisdom casts doubt on the success of many of the modern happiness-seeking techniques being practised so enthusiastically on the beach and in the shops. It also questions whether modern friendships even deserve the name. What is the key to lasting happiness according to wisdom? There are two very important keys associated with wisdom. The first is the key to happiness itself. It is that happiness is a by-product. If you seek it directly, you rarely find it. Instead you must seek something else, usually a virtuous or good life, the path of duty and then all other things will be added unto you including deep and lasting happiness.

This lesson is not difficult to appreciate even today. A little self-reflection shows that the pleasures on the beach or in the bars are not very reliable. A day can dawn which seems to promise so much. It is a day off work, when we can do what we like, when we have money, when the sun is shining, when we have firm arrangements to meet good friends. And all these supposed conditions of happiness are fulfilled. We meet the friends. We do what we want. We buy what we want. The felicific calculations are just right. But it doesn't work out. And days when we have to do things we don't associate with happiness can, paradoxically, bring it.

There is a branch of psychology which investigates what makes people happy. There's no reason to accord its detailed findings – that country dancing is the most direct route to happiness or that women are happier than men – much credibility. But it does show that, according to people's own assessments, more and more money does not necessarily bring more happiness and since money is the opportunity to have more and more of what one thinks one wants, having more of what one wants does not necessarily bring happiness.

This elusive aspect of happiness, were it taken seriously, would have devastating results for most of modern society is built on the assumption that happiness can be directly sought. Individuals are encouraged to decide what it is they enjoy then seek as much of it as possible. Political ideologies seek to aid people in this quest. Behind all the talk about rights, justice, opportunity and higher standards lies the implication that the rights are to happiness, the justice about the fair distribution of happiness, the opportunities for happiness and the higher standards, standards of happiness. The words of wisdom in the dusty volumes in the little bookshop are a rebuke to everything the world outside "knows" about happiness.

Wisdom does not live in texts. It demands qualities of those who seek it

The second key is the key *to* wisdom. Wisdom is often thought to lie in texts such as those quoted above. The Bible is a text and so is Aristotle's *Ethics*. But texts do not, as some people suppose, *contain* wisdom. Even simple texts which are about mere information, texts such as mobile phone instruction manuals or restaurant menus won't work unless the reader has some basic knowledge already; and not just knowledge but a willing disposition. This is much more the case with wisdom texts. It may seem odd but to get any wisdom out of such a text you have to be already fairly wise.

You have, as I have mentioned, to be prepared to make an effort. You have, first of all, to value wisdom and seek it, to be well-disposed to it. Even this calls for certain virtues such as patience and humility. Then you have to be prepared to be part of the tradition that the text belongs to. Wisdom texts come from cultures and traditions. Readers who can't or won't learn the tradition simply will not get much from the text. And learning may not be purely an act of the intellect. It may involve a way of life or even a religious discipline. There is certainly one view of the Bible which asserts that it cannot be understood unless approached prayerfully and as part of a Christian community. Even if one does not go that far, wisdom involves the seeker of wisdom in being a certain sort of character and sympathizing with a tradition. A simple example: the text about Jonathan should, when read by the wise person, set off associations. The language, from the Authorized Version is very similar to that of the *Book of Common Prayer*. More particularly the ideas of friends' souls being knit is very similar to that of marriage partners being knit in the service for the Solemnization of Matrimony. Later we shall see that much wisdom literature considers friendship as more important than marriage and the family. It is certainly like it. That little phrase from Samuel sets off an important and far-reaching understanding of friendship – at least in the head of the man who is already wise.

Friendship cannot be manipulated to produce happiness

A lot of wisdom about a lot of things casts doubt on the value of calculating and instrumental thinking and behaviour. If happiness cannot be approached in a direct calculating way, buying this, doing that in order to get happiness, then friendship cannot be engineered in order to be happy. Not only won't such a friendship lead to happiness but it won't be a true friendship. Friendships are not undertaken for what one may get out of them but for themselves. This does not mean that they are not happy. Cicero points out that not only happiness but material advantage, money, a better job, can come from friendship but it may not be undertaken in order to seek these. For those who hold a high view of friendship, such as Aristotle, friendship is part of the life of virtue. It is not a peculiarly Greek or Christian view. Here is Coleridge writing of his friendship with Southey,

On what grounds...did I form friendship with him? Because our pursuits were similar, our final aspirations similar, and because I saw plainly, that compared with the mass of men Southey was pure in his Habits habitually indignant at oppression...Not that he was perfection; but because he was a far better man, than the vast majority of young men, whom I knew.[107]

Such a virtuous friendship may bring happiness but is not undertaken for it. Indeed it is not undertaken for any outcome. It is worthwhile in itself. It is what sociologists call expressive rather than functional.

True friendship: Aristotle, Cicero, Dr Johnson

Cicero called friendship,

Complete identity of feeling about all things divine and human, as strengthened by mutual goodwill and affection.[108]

A well-known book on traditional notions of friendship was appropriately titled *Other Selves.*[109] Friends, as the opening quotation from Aristotle says, love the best of themselves in the other and the other brings out the best in themselves. Friendship is a virtuous conspiracy. The virtues involved are loyalty, self-sacrifice, trust, a commitment to a shared idea of the good, and truth. Friends are never flatterers. Of course they keep confidences but they tell each other the truth about each other and thus learn the truth about themselves. Seneca says,

Speak as boldly with [your friend] as with yourself...Share with [him] at least all your worries and reflections...Why need I keep back any words in the presence of a friend?[110]

Of course there is an element of chance attraction in friendship. Montaigne writes,

If I were pressed to say why I love [him], I feel that my only reply could be: because it was he, because it was I.[111]

The Greek writers would want to say that what I found attractive was a similar disposition to virtue. Yet this virtue in friendship is no sourpuss Puritanism. Writing of a famously great friend Robert Lynd puts it thus:

> *We laugh with [Dr Johnson] because he engages our sympathies…he is the perfect boon companion…In him goodness becomes convivial and grandeur of soul took its ease in the tavern. In his conversation, virtue holds a carnival and wisdom is at once sociable and riotous.*[112]

The loss of something is a good way of measuring its value and the value of high friendship is well shown in, for instance, Saint Augustine's description of what he felt on the death of a friend,

> *Grief…torment…misery…All that we had done together was now a grim ordeal without him. My eyes searched everywhere for him, but he was not there to be seen. I hated all the places we had known together, because he was not in them…I wondered that he should die and I remain alive, for I was his second self.*[113]

Friendship is a way of practicing virtue: Newman

This high ideal of friendship is high partly because it is associated with goodness. But it is not just that we have to understand and subscribe to the virtues of fidelity, trust and self-sacrifice in order to be true friends, to be part of the tradition in which true friendship is rooted. It is that friendship provides a way of exercising the virtues, a practical way in which to be and do good. John Henry Newman puts it like this:

> *How absurd it is when writers…talk magnificently about loving the whole human race with a comprehensive affection, of being friends of all mankind…this is not to love men, it is but to talk of love. The real love of man must depend on practice…It is obviously impossible to love all men in any strict and true sense. What is meant by loving all men, is to feel well-disposed to all men, to be ready to assist them, and to act towards those who come our way, as if we loved them. We cannot love those about whom we know nothing; except indeed we view them in Christ, as the objects of his Atonement, that is, rather in faith than*

love. And love, besides, is a habit, and cannot be attained without actual practice, which on so large a scale is impossible.[114]

Because friendship is tied up with virtue there can be no bad friendship. C S Lewis, who otherwise was a great friend of friendship, is far from the only one to have had difficulties with this. Lewis wants first to defend friendship. It is neglected today (1960) he complains. He reminds his readers of the great Aristotelian and Ciceronian tradition and emphasizes that friendship is indeed a love, and it may be a good love. Friendship is more than companionship and clubability. It may start from them but it is based on the friends recognizing that they are "are on a common secret road", that they "see the same truth". This can be the moral content identified by Aristotle. Moreover friendship can be useful to society. In an age obsessed with sociological explanations of things, which explains history in terms of structural changes in the economy or culture, Lewis points out that the Romantic movement once was Mr Wordsworth and Mr Coleridge talking incessantly about a secret vision of their own. Communism, Tractarianism, Methodism, the movement against slavery, the Reformation, the Renaissance, might perhaps be said, without much exaggeration, to have begun in the same way.

But then come the problems. What can be the school of virtue can be the school of vice. The shared secret truth can be a lie and an evil lie at that. The delight in company and talk can be exclusive. Friendships can be sets, coteries, gangs, mutual admiration societies. Authority frowns on friendship because

Every real friendship is a sort of secession. It may be a rebellion of serious thinkers against accepted clap-trap or of faddists against accepted good sense…it makes good men better and bad men worse.[115]

It is ambivalent but always subversive.

Bad friendships are not friendships

These worries turn on the definition of friendship. If it is merely a shared secret interest then of course it is ambivalent. But if Lewis really follows the Athenian definition then "bad" friendships are not friendships at all but perversions of friendship, things which have the forms of friendship without the moral content. Of course friendships can go wrong and bad. And Lewis later touches on one way which, for Christians is especially worrying. This, unlike the "school for vice" worry, is true, almost by definition, for any friendship which forgets God.

Friends, says Lewis, tend to think that they have chosen each other or fallen together by fate. Not so,

> *A secret master of ceremonies has been at work. Christ, who once said to the disciples, "Ye have not chosen me, but I have chosen you," can truly say to every group of Christian friends, "You have not chosen one another but I have chosen you for one another." The friendship is not a reward for our discrimination and good taste in finding one another out. It is the instrument by which God reveals to each the beauties of all the others…At this feast…let us not reckon without our Host.*[116]

This is a legitimate worry but only a worry. Again, Lewis goes too far. Friendships, to most orthodox Christians, are not divinely determined. Indeed God is the host but He does not compel the guests to come to the feast. In forming friendships we do discriminate and exercise taste and act freely. In good friendships, in true friendships as in any other good action, we do so by cooperating with the divine intention – but operating nevertheless.

What C S Lewis says about friendships can be said about families or even churches. They too can become cliques. They can become exclusive, wrapped up in themselves, oblivious, even subversive of divine authority.

The usual piece of knowledge cited on bad friends is E M Forster's remark that, if called on to betray friend or country, he would hope he would have the courage to betray his country.[117] Aristotle, as Andrew Sullivan rightly remarks,[118] would have found this remark "nonsensical. Cicero would have found it contemptible". Both would have been right.

> *A true friend will never put his friend in a moral dilemma; he will not ask him to do what is wrong or ask him to place their friendship before the common good, or demand that he lie for him, or make excuses for him.*

Sullivan then quotes Cicero:

Alliance of wicked men not only shouldn't be protected by a plea of friendship, but rather they should be visited with summary punishment of the severest kind, so that no one may think it permissible to follow even a friend when waging war against his own country;

and Aelred:

Love is shameful and unworthy of the name of friendship wherein anything foul is demanded of a friend....We should detest the opinion of those who think that one should act in behalf of a friend in any way detrimental to faith and uprightness. For it is no excuse for sin, that you sin for the sake of a friend.

Friendship protects rather than corrupts virtue in public life

It follows from the goodness of friendship that it should be welcome in the public arena. The classical writers, especially the Romans, did not see friendship as a source of corruption in business or politics. Quite the reverse; they thought it was dangerous to try to lead the virtuous life on one's own. One needs a friend to keep one on the straight and narrow. The same point can be found in Shakespeare and in Burke:

Therefore it is meet
That noble minds keep ever with their likes;
For who so firm that cannot be seduced?[119]

The only method which has ever been found effectual to preserve any man against the corruption of nature and example, is an habit of life and communication of councils with the most virtuous and public-spirited men of the age you live in. Such a society cannot be kept without advantage or deserted without shame.[120]

I remember an old scholastic aphorism, which says, "that the man wholly detached from others, must be either an angel or a devil". When I see in any of these detached gentlemen of our times the angelic purity, power, and beneficence, I shall admit them to be angels. In the mean time we are born only to be men. We shall do enough if we form ourselves to be good ones. It is therefore our business carefully to cultivate in our minds, to rear to the most perfect vigour and maturity, every sort of generous and honest feeling that belongs to our nature. To bring these dispositions that are lovely in private life into the service and conduct of the commonwealth; so to be patriots, as not to forget we are gentlemen. To cultivate friendships, and to incur enmities. To have both strong, but both selected: in the one, to be placable; in the other, immoveable.[121]

Friendship, the basis of academic and intellectual life

In fact friendship can sustain high standards in business and political life. It is, or was, a crucial ingredient of university life. Over the last two centuries many successful and justifiably famous men have passed through the universities. Re-reading their biographies, it is so often made clear that there they fell in with this or that individual or group, and that this friendship was significantly responsible for their education and success. Going up to a university used to mean much more than attending lectures, reading books, writing essays and passing exams. It used to mean joining a community and acquiring its values. A student might learn to appreciate literature or discover a vocation for the church not only by book reading but by seeing love of literature or Christian ministry exhibited in the life of a tutor. The friendship that can grow up between tutor and taught when they find similar passions and convictions can provide the incentives for a further pursuit of knowledge and practice. Noel Annan in his study *The Dons* notices of the charismatic John Henry Newman, while at Oxford.

> *[He] held himself responsible for his students' conduct. He was unique in treating them as his friends, and those who responded hung on his every word.*[122]

Many a student has become a Christian or a Marxist, a lawyer or a biologist because of a person. That person may attract others to him and his ideas through his brilliance of thought or argument, through his courage, sincerity, kindness or some other quality. And he may not and does not need to become a friend for the attraction to happen. But in many cases friendship, of a sort, does ensue and plays its part.

Friendships also exist between academic staff. And some of them are not just friendships of two or more academics but academic friendships. A well-known one was that small group called the Inklings just before, during and after the Second World War at Oxford. It consisted of C S Lewis, his brother, J R Tolkien and Charles Williams and some others. They met, read from the books they were writing and drank beer. In 1933 Tolkien wrote that his friendship with Lewis,

Besides giving constant pleasure and comfort, has done me much good from the contact with a man at once honest, brave, intellectual – a scholar, a poet, and a philosopher – and a lover, at least after a long pilgrimage, of Our Lord.

This and what follows is from Humphrey Carpenter's *The Inklings.*[123]

Lewis himself describes the beginning of the friendship as based on a recognition that they were both fired by the same enthusiasm for "northern" myths. The friendship starts when someone who till then has believed his feelings to be unique cries out,

What? You too? I thought I was the only one.

This knowledge that someone sees the world as you do is, says Leo Strauss, central to intellectual endeavour and the pursuit of truth.

The philosopher cannot lead an absolutely solitary life because legitimate "subjective certainty" and the "subjective certainty" of the lunatic are indistinguishable. Genuine certainty must be "inter-subjective". The classics were fully aware of the essential weakness of the mind of the individual. Hence their teaching about the philosophic life is a teaching about friendship: the philosopher is, as a philosopher, in need of friends.[124]

Friendship has been identified too as the ingredient that makes armies work. So many heroes are such not out of loyalty to their leaders but to their comrades. This public character of friendship leads to another characteristic that, in the wise society, friendship as a public good will be publicly acknowledged.

And last, this good, public institution, friendship should not have to play second fiddle to other institutions. It is as important as, for instance, the family. As Euripides has one character say,

A true friend is worth 10,000 relatives.[125]

So wisdom, the wisdom of Aristotle, Cicero, of the Old and New Testaments, of Dr Johnson, JH Newman and others gives us a picture of friendship that is deep, broad and fundamental, good in itself but also a public good. What does modern knowledge have to say about it?

Modern knowledge ignores friendship

The answer is simply, "Not much". There is just very little written about friendship today. Andrew Sullivan puts it succinctly,

> *We hardly talk about [friendship]...The twentieth century has seen almost no theoretical exploration of friendship, no exposition of what it means, no defense of it, or even attack on it. Those modern writers who have ventured to deal with friendship have done so in passing...One has to journey far...back, to ancient and mediaeval times, to glimpse a world where this relationship was given its full due and seen as something worth examining in its own right – as a critical social institution, as an ennobling moral experience, as an immensely delicate but essential interplay of the virtues required to sustain a fully realized human being.* [126]

It might be argued that the English, in particular, are not as given as some other cultures to theoretical knowledge or expertise. They have a tradition of amateurism which mocks elaborate, systematic and metaphysical knowledge. But even allowing for this, when one looks to find pragmatic, anecdotal, axiom-type knowledge on friendship, one finds little. Look in obituaries. Surely there one might expect to find mention of what his friends had meant to the deceased. It is just not there. One obituaries editor told me there are two reasons why it is not there. The first is that prolonged mention of a friendship might be read as indicating homosexuality or an illicit affair. The second is that obituaries writers did not know what to say about friendship.

Look in newspapers to see if there are surveys on the state of friendship, as there are on the state of almost anything else, and you will find nothing. Look in letters to and from advice columnists where you would expect to find the troubles and solutions of friends. There are indeed some letters mentioning friendship problems but the solutions are perfunctory. And, anyway, one should not press the amateuristic, anti-theoretical bias of the English too far. Take friendship's great rival, the family and family relationships. Substantial sections of psychology, sociology, ethics and social policy are taken up with family matters. Bookshops have shelves of books on sexual relationships, marriage and the family. Magazines and newspapers are obsessed with them. There are endless questionnaires and surveys about the state of them and reams of "expert" advice on how to improve them. There is simply nothing like this on friendship. This is not to say that friendship is unpopular:

94 per cent of young people regard having friends as very important or important...one per cent thought it unimportant. [127]

Modern thinking restricts and trivializes friendship

Friendship is very popular. But in the rare surveys which are done on what people think of it, what emerges is a very limited, shallow and restricted idea of friendship. There are odd places where something is written about it: greetings cards. And, at first sight they seem to have, given their few lines, quite a lot to say about it. The cards do have a special category of relationship called friendship. They don't confuse it with business or family relationships or even acquaintanceships. And the friends in the cards talk to each other of trust, shared pleasure, confidentiality and several other characteristics of friendship.

Today's people may not be able to talk precisely about friendship but they can recognize it and several of the qualities they associate with it follow classical lines. There are also some differences with classical definitions of friendship. Except in the odd card there is nothing that could be called a shared moral outlook. There is plenty of shared outlook but little on moral outlook. It may well be that exchanging cards on an occasion such as a birthday is not the right time for putting the world to right, though even that is a modern view. Perhaps a more interesting divergence from the classical understanding of friendship is that the cards are mostly about good times. Some mention hard times but the friendship itself is a happy, enjoyable thing. And that is what most modern people would expect of friendship. Classical authors, by contrast, are preoccupied with such matters as the sacrifices necessary for friendship or its cost. David and Jonathan's friendship exhibits a typically classical theme in the awful conflict of loyalties it presents.

Presumably modern friends have conflicts of loyalties between, for instance, what they owe to parents and what they owe to friends. Sexual attraction can cause mayhem among groups of friends and jealousy and betrayal are not unknown. But there is little of this in the cards. Classical writers also dwelt on the obligations of their sort of friends to tell the unpleasant truth to each other.

And this absence of harshness, this happiness, illustrated by smiling suns, is linked to another modern feature of the cards. They are largely about recreation, having a good time together outside work. There is little mention of work, politics, illness, public life or the economy. Again this seems thoroughly modern. Modern friendship takes place largely in recreational time. This also contrasts with especially Roman concepts of friendship. It further means that modern friendship does not appear very well-anchored in the unpleasant realities of life. There is much talk of trust and helping each other but the actual tasks this might call for, the actual practices it might lead to at work or in public life are difficult to get at. Modern friendship, in terms of practice, what people actually do, is centred on recreation. Hence the images in the cards of coffee mugs, chatting on the phone, toys, sailing boats, teddy bears, puppies with slippers, roses, thatched cottages, geraniums, suns, butterflies, sun hats, chocolate cake.

It is not quite true that modern academic knowledge has nothing to say about friendship. There is a small psychology of it but that too has a similar message to the cards. It is functionalist. It speaks of what friendship does for the friend, what friends get out of friendship. This is well captured in the title of the famous Dale Carnegie book, *How to win friends and influence people*.[128] But a more recent, respected psychologist, Steve Duck, can also spend time rehearsing the alleged beneficial functions of friendship. First there are the expectations.[129] Friends are expected to be honest and open, to share confidences, spend time with us in activities, repay debts and favours, engage in conversation, and not criticize each other in public. Steve Duck then gives a list of the functions of friendship. It gives a sense of belonging and reliable alliance. Emotional integration and stability, opportunities for communication about ourselves, physical support and support to our personalities. *How to win friends and influence people* is a variant on the same theme. It points out how people's personalities, success and income can be enhanced by the use – some might say, abuse – of their friends and friendship. Robert Bellah et al[130] have pointed out how psychologists view friendship as delivering psychic rather than material goods, feelings of self-worth, for example. All this of course is about the uses a friend can derive from "friendship". This is a long way from having a friendship for its own sake.

Steve Duck's equivalent in sociology is Graham Allan. He also emphasizes the two key characteristics of modern friendship as spending time together in recreation and exchanging and keeping confidences. He sees certain other functions for friendship. It can help in getting jobs, in getting advancement at work, in getting covering for oneself at work when one is ill or elderly, in times of difficulty or emergency. Friendship can give practical support as well as emotional meaning. But Allan is well aware that this, however welcome, is a long way from the classical understanding of friendship.[131]

Aristotle, we have seen, saw the best friendship not just as mutually useful or recreative but as a fusion of virtues, the high point of moral life. A friend, he says, is one who

Wishes good for his friend for his friend's sake.[132]

Friendship is ousted from politics, business and public life

There is one other place to look for contemporary advice on friendship. That is in the teaching on other institutions on which friendship might intrude. Two obvious ones are business and the family. The classical ideal can find no better foundation for business than friendship. The current teaching of business ethics is completely the opposite. Do not appoint friends. Do not share stock market knowledge with friends. Keep work and friendship apart. Moreover, since the highest virtue in modern business and public life is transparency and explicitness, and since friendship is by nature informal, keep friendship out of the office, out of government. This antipathy to friendship is also based on the assumption of equal rights. Friendship is preferential. We owe more to our friends than to other people. Whereas modern rights theory is egalitarian.

The old idea was that friendship helped business, politics, research, teaching, the professions and public life. The new idea is that they should shun it. Its proper place today is confined to recreation. As the greetings cards taught, it is about pleasure.

Friendship excluded by the exaltation of the family

The old teaching was also that friendship was as important, if not more so, than the family. Today, the family is exalted as the institution above all others. The modern family is a greedy institution, demanding ever more time and attention. A husband is expected to love, feel for, desire his wife and show it; he is also expected to be her companion and friend, and she his. Parents are expected to dote on their children, but also be their "friends", someone they can talk to as equals. The combination of romantic, tightly knit and friendly expectations is a tall order and, some might argue, a very confused and contradictory one. But that is not our concern. What are the implications for friendship? The modern ideals of life centre on the family and other forms, such as friendship, are squeezed out. This does not mean we actually spend more time in the family which, for a variety of reasons, is failing.

Modern "wisdom" gives no ideal, no guidance, no public image of friendship, so friendship is weak when it comes into conflict with the family. Which man today would have the courage or the wisdom to argue that sometimes he has duties to be with his friends in the club or pub rather than bathing his children at home? We certainly make what we call friendships but because we don't know how to do so properly and have little guidance, but harbour sophisticated social expectations, what we actually get are bogus friendships. Whether one accepts this or not, it would be a blind person who did not see that families can come into rivalry with and conflict with friendships. And our modern knowledge of friendship is so weak that even to understand this tension we are better off listening to the wisdom of the past. Samuel Butler wrote in the nineteenth century:

A man's friendships are, like his will, invalidated by marriage – but they are no less invalidated by the marriage of his friends. The rift in friendship which invariably makes its presence on the marriage of either of the parties to it was fast widening [with the marriage of Ernest Pontifex to Ellen], as it no less invariably does, into the great gulf which is fixed between the married and the unmarried.[133]

Charles Lamb is even more caustic. He warns any friend of a groom,

If the husband with whom you have lived on a friendly footing before marriage, – if you did not come in on the wife's side, – if you did not sneak into the house in her train, but were an old friend in fast habits of intimacy before their courtship was as much as thought of – your tenure is precarious – before a twelve-month shall roll over your head, you shall find your old friend gradually grow cool and altered towards you, and at last seek opportunities of breaking with you.[134]

If friends are lost at marriage, they are also lost at divorce, when they must take one side, and lost again at re-marriage. Much has been said about the damage modern marriage has done to the family. Yet modern knowledge has nothing to say about the damage it has done to friendship. It does not care.

Modern philosophy has no interest in friendship

This chapter started with a quotation from the philosopher, Aristotle, who regards friendship as, possibly, the best thing in the world. What do modern philosophers, the practitioners of the knowledge that might claim to be closest to wisdom, make of friendship? Most show no interest in it. Many modern philosophers are concerned with the consequences of actions especially for happiness and, as we have seen, friendship is not concerned with consequences. It is done for itself. Others are concerned with justice in the sense of equality or at least in the sense of universalisable rules, things we ought to do for all men. Friendship is obviously and blatantly anti-egalitarian. I prefer my friend to other people and love him more than them. It is modern "rights" based philosophy which undergirds the sort of business ethics that cannot abide the notion of advantaging a friend. Applied modern philosophy would drive friendship out of government, business and the public arena where Aristotle thought it most essential. These applications of modern philosophy, especially those centred on equality, are loosely "left-wing". The exaltation of the family, to the exclusion of friendship, is, loosely, "right-wing". The point is that neither socialists nor conservatives, neither the representatives of public life nor those of the family, have any time for friendship.

All the expertise, indeed all the wisdom in the world, cannot make a single friendship. But friendship needs public standards, wisdom and conventions. True friendship needs to be publicly understood, publicly displayed and publicly applauded, and bogus trivial and restricted friendship, the sham that passes for friendship today, needs to be publicly noted and belittled. Friendship and modern society will only recover when they take seriously traditional wisdom and the demands not just to intellect but to virtue that wisdom makes.

CHAPTER 5

Raising children

John and Karen Danford

We know that we have made no discoveries, and we think that no discoveries are to be made, in morality; nor many in the great principles of government, nor in the ideas of liberty, which were understood long before we were born, altogether as well as they will be after the grave has heaped its mould upon our presumption, and the silent tomb shall have imposed its law on our pert loquacity.[135]

More child disorder as expertise increases

Because in raising children we don't get much chance to learn from our mistakes, there seems to be no real possibility of expertise in this most complex of undertakings. Perhaps this is why traditional wisdom for so long maintained its authority. But today many parents – especially well-educated and affluent parents – don't raise their children, preferring (because they are so busy) to rely on child experts. The results – at least to teachers (like us) – are frightening. Nothing in everyday life today is done so badly as child rearing, whatever the reason. Let us begin with that.

In 1992 our oldest child was ten, and we made a discovery: we didn't like most of our friends' children (nor, for that matter, our children's friends), and we didn't see eye to eye with the schools, the Boy Scouts, the Little League, or the other groups to which our children were drawn. When we went to pick up our son from an end-of-season baseball team celebration at a local hamburger joint, it seemed odd that there was no one in the place except the boys, some parents and two employees. Odder still, the boys were running around, chairs were knocked over, food and paper were on the floor, and no one was doing anything about it. Parents sat chatting, while two young Hispanic employees crouched behind the counter, watching in dismay and disbelief. Our son, seeing the disapproval on his mother's face, tried unsuccessfully to prevent her from saying "don't throw food" or "pick up that chair". The young man and woman behind the counter implored her to stop the kids from throwing ice, as someone could get hurt and they would lose their jobs.

It might have been understandable had the boys been acting up with no adults around. But the parents sat enjoying themselves while their children trashed a public restaurant, tyrannizing one another and the employees. The social class of these barbarians is interesting mainly because the parents are among the most successful and highly educated people in the world. They believe in science and progress, and have probably read more books by child-rearing experts than anyone, anywhere, at any time. Yet some of their children are on mind-altering drugs like Ritalin and Prozac to make them manageable, and most of the rest are simply intolerable. Endless articles and television programmes decry the decreasing civility in our society, even as experts produce more books and programmes to discuss what should be done. At one Internet site called "AOL Parenting" recently, 85.5 per cent of 85,827 respondents said children were more "spoiled" today than ever before. This fact is displayed along with other nasty titbits about parents spoiling children, but without a hint of honesty about what causes the problem and what should be done.

What is different now: prosperity, equality?

People offer a variety of explanations for what many agree is the bad behaviour – or at least bad manners – of young people today. First, two socio-economic trends may be part of the explanation. People in advanced industrial societies are richer than human beings have ever been, and there is an old saying: *Curis acuens mortalia corda* (unfortunately it's in Latin because it comes from Virgil, the great Latin poet) which teaches that our wits are sharpened – we work harder – when we are spurred by necessity.[136] Perhaps we attend more to good behaviour when we feel the costs of bad behaviour more, and our prosperity works as a sort of cushion, preventing us from feeling any bad effects from rude or inconsiderate or churlish conduct.

It would be difficult to deny that another trend in advanced industrial (more or less democratic) societies – increasing equality of circumstances – has an effect on behaviour. Equality of conditions (as de Tocqueville called it) means that we aren't accustomed to looking up to authorities. There can't be a teacher alive today who has not heard a student say something like "I'm entitled to my opinion, and it's worth as much as anybody else's opinion". The relativism this engenders has important effects when it comes to regulating conduct by moral authority or even rules (especially norms sanctioned by tradition). Carried to its logical conclusion, egalitarianism undermines even parental authority. Who, after all, is to say the judgement of a teacher or a father is superior to that of a sixteen-year-old, or, for that matter, a ten-year-old?

The sixties and the sexual revolution

Many observers believe that today's ills should be blamed on the rise of the counter-culture more than a generation ago, in the 1960s, when student protests and street demonstrations broke out in many cities and universities in the advanced industrial countries (and most authorities – such as university administrators – crumbled very quickly after some token resistance). Some of this ferment was associated with the Vietnam War, but there was also a more general rebellion against authority of any kind, including traditional moral prescriptions of all sorts ("respect your elders", "be polite", "dress appropriately", etc). The 1960s counter-cultural revolution even had a philosophical or at least ideological side: it meant to throw out antiquated beliefs such as the belief in human nature, which was to be replaced by the sophisticated view that human beings are "socially constructed" beings. The differences between men and women, for example, are not grounded in nature; such differences are merely artefacts of various social structures (mostly oppressive and patriarchal structures, which it is necessary to overthrow).

Modern science and technology replace religious and moral wisdom

These views, of course, play a major role in how we raise our children, but they have a much longer pedigree. The rebellion against manners began with Rousseau in 1750 (if not earlier) – with the notion that children are innocent, while society is corrupt – and many other such views originated in the eighteenth and nineteenth centuries, in the great reaction against first the Church, and later against Enlightenment rationalism. Thinkers of the Enlightenment claimed to be discovering the real nature of things – including human nature – by means of scientific inquiry. These two philosophical traditions, the romantic, natural view and the rational, scientific view of human beings, have a long legacy in educational theory and child-raising literature. According to Christopher Lasch, by the beginning of the 1920s "allegedly outmoded concepts such as guilt and sin" were converted to medical concepts and became the province of doctors and social pathologists who then monopolized their "treatment". Everyone from psychiatrists to advertisers

claimed to understand the "needs" of the young better than their parents did... Only modern science and technology, it appeared could provide the growing child with the proper nutrition, the proper medical care, and the social skills he needed in order to function in the modern world.[137]

In sex, knowledge replaces rules

Another development sometimes associated with the 1960s deserves to be singled out, the so-called "sexual revolution", or the assault on traditional moral restrictions on sexual gratification (which confined sexual relations to a man and a woman in marriage). The new view – that sexual gratification is almost always healthy and should not be restricted to marriage or even to adult heterosexual relations – is best summed up in the slogan, "if it feels good, do it". Aside from the obvious connection (at least traditionally!) between sex and children, however, what does this have to do with raising children? Many parents today feel uncomfortable exercising authority. They want, instead, to be their children's friend. Setting limits is antithetical to their world view. Gone with the taboos against certain kinds of risky behaviour is any sense of shame. Where traditional wisdom taught that sexual promiscuity is dangerous, children today are taught the "facts of life" not by reticent parents but by professionals. Armed with this knowledge, and supplied with condoms, they are expected to be sexually active at a much earlier age. Negative consequences such as disease, pregnancy, or even emotional problems, can be treated by medical and psychological experts with no stigma attached.[138]

The sexual revolution was also associated with the feminist movement, which aimed at liberating women from patriarchal oppression. In reality feminists sought liberation from nagging mothers (the purveyors of traditional *mores*) and inconvenient biology. Feminist progress has resulted in more and more women taking jobs outside the home. Feminist success has thus meant that the task of raising children – a stronger word is needed for a project that takes 16 hours a day for many years – has increasingly been farmed out to a new class of child care experts. These well-meaning folks have an affinity for hare-brained schemes and crackpot theories, and, not coincidentally, as their failures have become ever more obvious, we are seeing more recourse to the pharmaceutical management of unruly children.

The experts

Do people really raise their children according to instructions or recipes from books written by experts? We don't know. But the number of such books is huge, and presumably someone is buying them and at least hoping to profit from them. We will treat the books and the experts as the same thing since, by and large, books on child-raising all make claims about the expertise of their authors, naturally enough, generally supported not by evidence in the form of "children successfully raised by the methods presented in this manual" but by credentials in the form of initials (MA, PhD, MD, etc). This of course begs the question to which this book is devoted. Bill Cosby, a comedian, was probably correct when he said

> *You know the only people who are always sure about the proper way to raise children? Those who've never had any.*[139]

Comedians, like the fool in *King Lear*, are among the only public figures who can speak truth to power on the subject of parents and children today.

At any rate, if people do raise their children according to books by experts, it is very difficult to summarize what the books teach, since there are so many fads and trends. Traditional notions of authority, of right and wrong conduct, proper manners, and the kind of discipline that really works, are clearly not very popular. Parents, we are assured, should teach their children values, but all values are equal (except those that are politically incorrect), and simultaneously children are urged not to be judgemental. It sometimes seems as if the only virtue valued today is tolerance. At the library, on one shelf is a book with advice for raising children in a lesbian "family", next to *In Defense of Masochism* next to William Bennett's *The Broken Hearth* about the breakdown of the traditional family. As Bruno Bettelheim observed,

> *Most advice on child-rearing is sought in the hope that it will confirm our prior convictions. If the parent had wished to proceed in a certain way but was made insecure by opposing opinions of neighbors, friends or relatives, then it gives him great comfort to find his ideas seconded by an expert.*[140]

This is from a book entitled, rather astoundingly, *Family Wisdom, the 2000 Most Important Things Ever Said About Parenting, Children and Family Life*. The editor, a "leading consultant on education, parenting and work-life issues", compiled 2000 entries spanning centuries and written by poets, philosophers, parents and experts. At least two thirds of the advice, however, is from psychologists, psychiatrists, social workers or educators, arranged by topic (ranging from bedtime to women's work choices), with no judgement made about anything and with entries contradicting one another. According to child psychologist Lawrence Kutner,

> *Our species successfully raised children for tens of thousands of years before the first person wrote down the word "psychology". The fundamental skills needed to be a parent are within us.*[141]

Six entries later we read:

> *Many people operate under the assumption that since parenting is a natural adult function, we should instinctively know how to do it – and do it well. The truth is, effective parenting requires study and practice like any other skilled profession.*[142]

What rings most true here is that family "wisdom" is a complicated affair because there is no one way to raise children, or as my mother used to say, what works for one child doesn't always work for another. Anyone who has more than one child learns this from the day the second is born. This doesn't stop psychologists in their quest for scientifically verifiable explanations for how we become what we are or from encouraging others to apply their theories. Susan Ginsberg, at least, does not pretend to have any answers – we can choose what we like and disregard the rest. The experts may claim to speak authoritatively, but they have little control over what we do (unless we have a run-in with the schools). This is very different from traditional ways of transmitting wisdom about child-rearing. You can throw out a book that makes you feel guilty, but you can't get rid of a grandmother or mother-in-law so easily. Another benefit of expert advice is that it absolves us of responsibility – if the experts were wrong, I can't be blamed.

Anyone watching trends in child-rearing advice can't help but notice that much research in the last decades – from the original claim that "quality time" is more important than quantity of time – has been aimed at relieving guilt and anxiety, especially about day care or divorce, or mothers working outside the home. Thus we hear that staying home or staying married can be harmful to children if parents are unhappy or dissatisfied. Funny how self-esteem was not a big issue when parents took for granted they were both needed to provide the love, guidance and security that every child needs, and at least one of those persons needed to be around to supervise a child's conduct. As my mother also used to say, the only people who really care about a child's character and conduct are the parents.

Two kinds of child-raisers

As in so many things, there is a political dimension to the general disagreement about how to raise children. Those who are generally satisfied with their lives – their achievements, their prospects, their material position, the state of their souls – are inclined to think their parents raised them in the right way, and try to follow the prescriptions and patterns passed on by the older generation. Such people are, of course, inclined to "conserve" what they think has worked well in the past. We all know people like this, and we also know those who are less happy with themselves or their worlds.

Modern psychology leads most of us to believe that if something is wrong, there must be a cause buried deep in the past. Some deficiency in one's early years – a cold or distant mother, an abusive father, too much sibling rivalry, favouritism – must explain whatever is wrong now. Those who blame the past are not likely to think there is much worth conserving, and they seek new and improved ways to bring up children: their attitude is progressive. The old ways should be discarded because they were the product of an age that was benighted (bigoted, superstitious, patriarchal and oppressive). For example, Dr John Gray expresses a sentiment found in many books:

> *Today we are faced with the challenge of reinventing parenting. Instead of assuming responsibility to mold our children into responsible and successful adults, it is becoming increasingly apparent that our role as parents is only to nurture what is already there... Traditional parenting skills and approaches that were appropriate in the past will not work for children today. Children are different. They are more in touch with their feelings and thus more self-aware. With this shift in awareness, their needs have changed as well.*[143]

Does this mean we should be nurturing a child to become an axe murderer, if that is already in his soul? He is, as we are told by other scientists, already genetically programmed.

Traditional wisdom about raising children

In any complicated human endeavour, especially one as universal as raising children, there are truths that come to be known through experience, and are transmitted from one generation to another in many ways, most of which are informal. This wisdom cannot be assembled in a book or place, because it is not known by one person, or group of persons, at any given time. It could be said to be contained in practices. The old wisdom about raising children was rooted in a belief that there is a human nature, and that human beings must be tamed, or civilized. The things that work have been winnowed from experience over time and are based in common sense. "Latent wisdom" exists in the traditions that are passed on in practice and in sayings and stories. Traditional wisdom gives no explicit instructions, and carries with it no promise of success, but it is highly adaptable and, some would say, reliable.

We will try to identify the main elements of traditional wisdom as they are known to us from our own experience, and compare them to some of the advice given today by the experts. We believe that traditional wisdom begins, above all, from the premise that children are born tyrants (totally self-centred and demanding) with a potential for good, and must be civilized in order to become members of society. As one grandmother lamented, full-time mothers knew that

> *The buck stopped with us. Whatever we allowed we had to endure [whereas] today's parents couldn't stand to be around their toddlers 24 hours a day.*[144]

She suggests forcing parent and child to spend five days in a small apartment with few diversions so that

> *Maybe, given enough time, [parents] would learn how pleasant and rewarding it is to be the parent of a well-behaved child.*

Authority, shame and discipline

The first and most important lesson of traditional wisdom about raising children is that they must respect adults, especially their parents. In the Bible, a source of much traditional wisdom about human beings, the fifth of God's Commandments says:

> *Honour your father and your mother, that your days may be long in the land which the Lord your God gives you.*[145]

This is the first of God's Commandments regarding human relationships and the only Commandment with a promise. What is important is the disposition, the attitude we should have. It does not say love, or even obey your parents.[146] There is a sense of the imperfection of all human beings, including parents; but in honouring them, recognizing their status as parents, we recognize ourselves as links in a chain, connected through time to other generations, and through creation to something beyond ourselves. The attitude of respect and obligation is connected to authority – to the authorship of our lives – and commands our attention. This is what the Romans called *pietas*, piety, embodied in Aeneas, the Trojan founder of Rome who carried his father on his shoulders from the flames of Troy.[147] Without respect for those who gave us life, how can we respect each other, or even ourselves? Perhaps this is also a way of saying that parents should act with honour, as well.

Most religions focus on parents as the connection to the gods and one's ancestors. Implicit here is that our behaviour reflects not only on ourselves but our entire family. In *Ecclesiasticus* it is written:

> *For a man's glory comes from honouring his father, and it is a disgrace for children not to respect their mother.*[148]

And later,

> *Discipline your son and take pains with him, that you may not be offended by his shamelessness.*[149]

Shame is important for both parents and children in traditional societies. Mothers and fathers used to say "Have you no shame?" or "Don't embarrass us!" It is up to parents to make sure that children know what is appropriate behaviour which will serve them in adulthood:

> *Train up a child in the way he should go, and when he is old he will not depart from it.*[150]

But what if a child resists the voice of authority, is impervious to internal controls like shame or guilt, and continues to act in ways unacceptable in his society? Here traditional wisdom is pretty clear: the child requires disciplining, sometimes in the form of physical punishment.

> *One who spares his rod hates his child, but who loves him is diligent to discipline him*[151]

because

> *Folly is bound up in the heart of a child, but the rod of discipline drives it far from him.*[152]

This philosophy of "spare the rod and spoil the child", (disciplining a child out of love) is diametrically opposed to modern psychological theories, which claim that punishment does not work. Yet most parents know that without at least the reasonable threat of corporal punishment, they have no control. A screaming two-year-old does not listen to reason, or cease misbehaving from hugs and kisses – he stops only when he gets what he wants, in which case be believes he controls things, or after some punishment reminds him that he does not.

Despite the belief that spanking constitutes child abuse and teaches violence, just about every parent we know has resorted to strategic spanking (sometimes uttering: "This hurts me more than it hurts you"). Even the inventors of "Time-Out", the new, improved, non-violent solution to bad behaviour, admit that if a child leaves the appointed "time-out" location, "one swift swat across the buttocks" may be needed.[153] Not so long ago, misbehaving children could be swatted by school principals, and few deny that things were a lot more orderly. Today the single most common teacher complaint is about the lack of discipline. Yet parents and teachers are advised to negotiate contracts with children, ignore inappropriate behaviour, and reinforce positive behaviour: Avoid anything that might damage a child's self-esteem or repress creativity. The result has been disastrous. Schools and day-care centres are still faced with unruly children, now free to tyrannize everyone.[154] In desperation, we resort increasingly to nonsensical "no tolerance" policies and, alarmingly, to drugs to control behaviour. Ritalin and Prozac have become "discipline in pill form". The quick fix is very tempting to parents who insist there is nothing wrong with their child, or their parenting. As one columnist asked recently,

Are we really prepared to define childhood as an ailment, and medicate it until it goes away?[155]

Teaching about good and evil

"Positive parenting" begins from the Rousseauian premise that children are born innocent and good. If they do not always act that way, they simply require positive forms of behaviour modification (or drugs) to control their inconvenient impulses. The experts seem to reject the belief that the world is a dangerous place with evil people in it. In contrast, traditional forms of upbringing relied quite heavily on negative images to warn children about evil both in the world and in themselves. Fairy tales and warning stories conveyed through the imagination a sense of good and bad on many levels. Parents might say: "don't swim for an hour after eating" or "don't play with sticks, you'll poke someone's eye out". These warnings were not always literally true – they were intended to heighten a sense of caution, an awareness that bad things can happen, and that one should avoid potentially dangerous situations. Today, psychologists label such statements as fear-mongering, since they may repress a child's need to explore and experience the world. There is a prevailing belief that negative images induce negative behaviour ("the violence in, violence out" theory).[156]

Parents increasingly worry about scaring children and try to protect them from violent, horrific depictions of evil, such as are found in the original Grimm's *Fairy Tales, Harry Potter,* or even some Walt Disney movies. Fairy tales embody the folk wisdom, and do indeed use horrific images of evil to help children understand the world. Bruno Bettelheim explained how children are equipped better to deal with the world through such stories:

> *There is a widespread refusal to let children know that the source of much that goes wrong in life is due to our very own natures – the propensity of all men for acting aggressively, asocially, selfishly, out of anger and anxiety. Instead we want our children to believe that, inherently, all men are good.*[157]

The message that fairy tales convey is that

> *A struggle against severe difficulties in life is unavoidable, is an intrinsic part of human existence – but that if one does not shy away, but steadfastly meets unexpected and often unjust hardships, one masters all obstacles and at the end emerges victorious.*[158]

As everyone knows, stepmothers were often portrayed as selfish and evil, as in *Cinderella, Snow White* and *Hansel and Gretel,* so it is understandable that parents in a divorce culture would reject such imagery. Yet both common sense and much research confirm that unrelated adults entrusted with the care of children are the most common abusers. In response, other experts have sought to show that natural parents are equally abusive.

Modern child-rearing experts prefer to avoid fairy tales, which they see as superstitious and ignorant relics of the pre-rational past. Neither in transmission nor in interpretation are stories subject to expert supervision, because they give too much play to imagination. The experts look for causal explanations, and may resort to such "re-educative" treatments as RET, "rational-emotive-therapy".[159] Fairy tales work in the opposite way by providing unreal situations that represent our fears, teach moral lessons, and may even entertain at the same time.

One may read or hear a fairy tale many times and glean different life lessons from it at different times. What an adult sees in a story may be quite different from what a child sees. For example, *The Frog Prince* tells the story of a beautiful, spoiled daughter who loses her golden ball, makes promises to an ugly frog who helps her retrieve it, and then tries to break her promises because he is so repulsive. Her father, the king, makes her keep her promises, which she grudgingly does, until she finally throws the frog against the wall in total disgust. At that point a spell is broken; the frog is transformed into a handsome prince, whom she marries, and his faithful servant who suffered with him is freed from the iron bands that bound his breaking heart. Our daughter thinks this story is about not trusting appearances; her mother thinks it is about keeping promises, and showing that father knows best. One prominent sociologist thinks it is about women civilizing men, even if grudgingly, as orchestrated by the hidden mother-witch who cast the original spell.[160]

Caring for others and sexual differences

In most fables and fairy tales, the lessons learned are relatively simple, though not always direct. In *The Little Red Hen*, for example, the selfish, lazy animals who do not help the hen make a cake still get to enjoy it once she escapes from the big bad wolf, who, incidentally, is only trying to find food for his family. Is the lesson that it pays to be lazy? Children may think so on a rational level, but they can also recognize laziness in the barn animals, they see the industry, service and wit of the little red hen, and vicariously delight in celebrating together when evil is overcome.

We are fond of another story that teaches children about perseverance and serving others, *The Little Engine that Could*.[161] The little train full of toys breaks down, and none of the available big engines will help pull her over the mountain. Finally a little blue switching engine rises to the occasion, struggling mightily by saying "I think I can, I think I can…" until she reaches the other side of the mountain where the children get their toys. Of course, parents like to repeat this to children when encouraging them to keep on trying. But the story is also about serving others; the engine that helps the children is referred to with the feminine pronoun and the big arrogant, strong or tired engines are given male voices.

Embedded in both these stories are references to sexual differences which modern parents might not find politically correct. Sexual differences, however, are a large part of traditional wisdom about human beings. The old expression "boys will be boys" is still heard today, but its meaning has changed. Now it is used as an excuse, as if to say nothing can be done about boys acting out, being aggressive, or not concentrating well. Probably it used to mean that boys need tougher measures to keep them in line.

In recent studies claiming that girls suffer low self-esteem, are at risk in schools, and therefore need special attention, ideological researchers ignore the facts about differences between girls and boys that anyone with siblings or children would take for granted. First, they assume that you can measure self-esteem in a poll by having children respond to statements such as "I am happy the way I am", as if most, or even some, children take such surveys seriously. Christina Hoff Summers doubts the effectiveness of the polls, but claims that even if we were to assume that the results were accurate, it doesn't necessarily mean that girls have low self-esteem – it may mean simply that girls mature earlier than boys and are more realistic in their self-assessment at a younger age.[162] These studies illuminate one of the most egregious ways experts are trying to remake human nature according to their own theories. Since traditional wisdom is based on real experience, not controlled scientific studies, it is less likely to distort the truth; such distortions would not survive the test of time.

Manners, habits and self-confidence

Modern "positive parenting" is determinedly child-centred, focusing on children's needs so as to help them "discover and express their true selves". Traditional wisdom focused on helping children grow up (and on shaping children who can be with adults while they are growing up). In a recent piece posted on the Internet, entitled "Excuse me...; The Decline of Manners", commentator John Derbyshire, father of a six- and nine-year-old, makes this observation:

> *Children no longer have a clue how to address adults outside their family. Call me reactionary if you like, but I am really not willing to accept anything other than "Mr Derbyshire" or "Sir" from anyone less than college age. I rarely hear either. The creepy thing is that the neighbor kids know there is something wrong here. They mumble and drop their eyes when getting my attention: "Excuse me, er, Mister, er..." They know there is a way to address me, but they don't know what it is.*[163]

We have had the same experience, and in fact sometimes our own friends undercut our insistence to our children that adults are to be addressed as Mr or Mrs. ("But Mom, she told me to call her Elizabeth.") Father John Piderit SJ, former president of Loyola University, Chicago, told us he used to conduct "manners classes" for college students, who received the informal (and voluntary) lessons with gratitude. They told him they found social relations much easier and more pleasant when they were confident about their table manners and didn't have to wonder how to address someone. This has been known for centuries, or at least since Philip Dormer Stanhope, the 4th Earl of Chesterfield, published his letters of advice and instruction to his son and grandson in the eighteenth century.[164]

Manners – mere manners, as some would say – have been under assault not just since the 1960s, but since 1750, when Jean-Jacques Rousseau attacked the Enlightenment's emphasis on "civility and good taste" which he believed antithetical to genuine virtue.

> *Civilized peoples, cultivate talents: happy slaves, you owe to them that delicate and refined taste on which you pride yourselves; that softness of character and urbanity of customs which make relations among you so amiable and easy; in a word, the semblance of all the virtues without the possession of any.*[165]

Even defenders of manners allow that "civil behaviour" has about it a whiff of hypocrisy. As John Derbyshire notes,

> *Better a false "Good morning" than a sincere "Go to hell", ran the old Yiddish saying. Less and less people [sic] agree with that.*[166]

The traditional wisdom was perhaps best captured in La Rochefoucauld's celebrated maxim,

> *Hypocrisy is the tribute vice pays to virtue.*

We know how we ought to act toward one another, and sometimes we pretend (we greet politely, even when we are ill-disposed) because if we showed all our rough edges it might be difficult to live with other people. But even such mild hypocrisy is objectionable to those who believe we are all good by nature, and that in the perfect social order toward which we are progressing we can all be honest, all the time. (Another enemy of polished manners – especially of respectful forms of address – is the egalitarian ethos which regards all human beings as equal at all times: children and adults, for example, should use first names when addressing each other.)

But perhaps manners are not merely the icing on the cake. Miss Manners, the noted etiquette columnist, penned a wonderful article ten years ago called "The World's Oldest Virtue". In it she suggested that manners are the foundation on which all moral behaviour rests. When a child learns manners he is above all learning to think of "the other". Even the magic words, "please" and "thank you", the saying of which we struggle to inculcate as habits in our children, are talismans of an internal admission that the world does not exist solely for the child's gratification.

> *The attitude that the wishes of others do not matter is exactly what manners are intended to counter. And no one has yet come up with a satisfactory substitute for family etiquette training in the earliest years of life to foster the development of the child in such principles of manners as consideration, cooperation, loyalty, respect, and to teach the child such etiquette techniques as settling disputes through face-saving compromise. Within the family, the manners that are needed (although not always in evidence) are those associated with responsibility and compassion, rather than individuality and strict justice: care of the*

helpless, respect for elders and for authority, allotment of resources on the basis of need, empathy with the feelings of others, the accommodation of differences.[167]

Wisdom and childhood

She also notes:

The schools are not able to teach these principles, however valiantly they may try, because a mannerly attitude and etiquette skills are prerequisites for learning anything at all in a school setting.[168]

Evidence for this is only too ubiquitous in the experience of any sentient adult not blinded by progressive ideology.

Rather than taking the trouble to correct children and teach them proper conduct, adults now act more like children. They themselves may never have learned manners, and in trying to please children have hastened to abandon their role as superiors. Frederic Hegel identified the disastrous effect this would have on children and civil society over a century ago:

The necessity for education is present in children as their own feeling of dissatisfaction with themselves as they are, as the desire to belong to the adult world whose superiority they divine, as the longing to grow up. The play theory of education assumes that what is childish is itself already something of inherent worth and presents it as such to the children; in their eyes it lowers serious pursuits, and the education itself, to a form of childishness for which children themselves have scant respect. The advocates of this method represent the child, in the immaturity in which he feels himself to be, as really mature and they struggle to make himself satisfied with himself as he is. But they corrupt and distort his genuine and proper need for something better, and create in him a blind indifference to the substantial ties of the intellectual world, a contempt of his elders because they have thus posed before him, a child, in a contemptible and childish fashion, and finally a vanity and conceit which feeds on the notion of its own superiority.[169]

Thus the inmates may truly be running the asylum now, as many suspect. So why do people keep having children, if they don't want to do the hard work to raise them? We have identified the modern faith in experts to correct whatever faults may occur, but we have also seen the results. Perhaps it is, after all, simply human nature.

CHAPTER 6

Playing games

Simon Green

The old games taught wisdom and developed character

At the Harrow School of the young Robert Peel, games were important yet apparently ramshackle affairs. They occupied a good deal of time; perhaps half of every day. However, compulsory team-sports barely existed at all. True, cricket and football (also hare-and-hounds) were offered to all boys. But they were cursorily organized and legendarily violent. Their contribution to victory at the battle of Waterloo can only have been in the cultivation of aggression amongst the upper classes.[170] Perhaps that is why many boys of the time declined to participate in them. One of the non-participants was Peel himself. Not that the future Prime Minister was an early couch potato. Far from it. Like most of his contemporaries he enjoyed fresh air, the countryside and outdoor pursuits. So, most afternoons he took himself off for a brisk walk in the local woods. But not just for a walk; invariably he returned to school with a bird or two which his more ingenuous peers thought he must have cleverly knocked down with a stone. In fact, unbeknownst to them – or indeed to the school authorities – he was covertly carrying on the same field sports which he had learned to love at home in Drayton. Gash completes the story:

> *Together with his inseparable companion, Robert Anstruther, he arranged for his guns to be kept for him during the term at the home of a cottager. When the two boys were thought to be peacefully rambling abroad, communing with nature like Byron beneath the immemorial elms, they were actually beating the distant hedgerows and coverts for…game, returning their weapons to sanctuary before walking back*

with their trophies to school.[171]

Wholly unsupervised, inevitably bloodthirsty in their aims and quite literally playing with fire, the two boys seem to have come to no great harm. Indeed, they may even have learned something crucial in their escapades. Peel himself certainly thought so. Indeed, in later life, he tended to the belief that illicit shooting taught him all he ever learned – of lasting value – at school. If so, Harrow had done at least part of its duty by him and for his country. He had refined his military skills and made fast some good friendships there. He would have served his country proud at Waterloo. He had also acquired some of the arts of dissemblance. These served him well in the career he actually followed.[172]

The Harrow of Winston Churchill, in the years immediately following Victoria's Golden Jubilee, was a rather different place.[173] And games played a very different role within its self-consciously reformed curriculum.[174] Most obviously, all known games were by then established firmly *within* the formal curriculum. Unauthorized shooting parties were emphatically a thing of the past. This was not because the boys had become less resourceful. It owed rather more to the unavoidable fact that untamed countryside was becoming increasingly difficult to find in the vicinity. And that was the direct result of the peculiarly relentless march of Harrow's playing-field provision. Amounting to just eight acres of contiguous property in 1845, this had risen nearly *twenty-fold*, to 146, by 1900. Contemporary Marlborough made do with just 68; Uppingham with 49.[175]

So much expensive investment could scarcely have been lightly undertaken. Thus it was far from coincidental that late-Victorian Harrow became something of a pioneer in compulsory games.[176] And not just any kind of games either; above all, team games. To be sure, vigorous individual activities were neither necessarily despised nor generally proscribed. Indeed, Churchill himself thrived at swimming and riding (and little else) during his time there.[177] But few contemporaries rated individual pursuits on a par with collective purposes. For the latter alone matched physicality with morality. One game emphatically so: cricket. Not for nothing did a popular history of the School, published during the 1880's, devote an entire chapter to this "noble sport".[178] This was because cricket epitomized not merely the strictly pedagogical but also the more general – social and moral –

possibilities of team games. These were not only various. They were also quite subtle. Certainly, they were never limited to the simple suppression of sexual vice or crude redirection of otherwise anarchic adolescent energies.[179] Indeed, they were only loosely related to mere bodily fitness. So much so that E E Bowen, the most plausibly cerebral of all contemporary Harrow sportsmen – and he was a footballer – never bothered to hide his contempt for "gym", dismissing it "as the mere Greek iambics of physical training".[180]

This was crucial. For Bowen, the goal was not (just) a healthy body; nor even (merely) a healthy mind. Like so many late Victorian educationalists, he meant not simply to ape but actually to go beyond the ancient, Olympian, ideal. His end was a morally-trained person. His point was that the best team games were the most efficient means to that end. This was partly because they acted as a "permanent corrective" to "laziness"; that was obvious. But it was more because they were also in their very ingenuousness a bulwark against "foppery and man-of-the-worldliness", that was less so. And it was more important. For it pointed to the capacity of games to make boys, otherwise increasingly cynical, admirably naive again. It was this inherent quality, that is, the essential good which came out of games pursued as games, that enabled them to breed "dignity, courtesy and co-operation" as a glorious side-effect of seemingly purposeless self-immersion.[181]

It followed that as such complex and indirect paths to virtue, games were not – could not be – strictly regulated modes of instruction. So participation was compulsory. But little else was. And supervision remained minimal. This was vital. Thus, for instance, the "science of cricket" might be inculcated into a boy. However, its practice demanded the *"exercise of due...and individual...resource"*.[182] That implied a fair measure of pleasure. But it also allowed for considerable personal suffering. Indeed, it almost courted injury. So much so that little or no attempt was made to take the danger out of otherwise "organized sports". More: part of the education gained from them was understood to arise out of that "contempt for pain" which the sportsmen displayed on the field of play.[183] Most of all, games constituted a form of activity which engaged masters and boys together. On occasion, literally for life: Bowen actually died on a Harrow football field at the age of sixty-five.[184] More usually they wielded their benevolent effects during the school years, simultaneously exacting and refining mutual concern and respect amongst juvenile and adult alike. That was why Bowen did not hesitate to celebrate games as *"the most valuable...part of the curriculum"*.[185] And this in a journal of education too.[186]

The new games minimize risk and maximize winning

Superficially, much of Churchill's Harrow remains in the contemporary sporting regime at the school. It retains extensive playing fields. Games are still compulsory. Team-sports predominate. Shooting survives. And sports and games occupy a great deal of *space* in the modern curriculum. But appearances deceive. In reality, Churchill's Harrow is as dead as Peel's. The current School prospectus places sports and games eighth and ninth respectively in the order of proffered activities; pointedly behind music, art, and drama.[187] Some thirty games are advertised. But no claims are made for the broader educational or moral purposes of any of them; save only through a lame observation from the present Rugby master that *"winning"* is best achieved by paying *"close attention...to individual and collective performances"*.[188] It is difficult not to conclude that this is an insight which many boys could have reached by themselves. Shooting is, of course, very strictly supervised. Perhaps this ensures that nothing animate now gets shot. More likely still, it means that the associated danger of the sport is kept to an absolute minimum.

This is, in fact, the case in all similar activities at the school. And there is very little peculiar about Harrow in this respect. Few contemporary schools dare to take the slightest risk with pupil safety in the wake of the Children Act. That is why most have now quietly removed all serious hazards from their military assault courses (sic); this – it should now go without saying – as protection against possible legal liability.[189] But some have gone far beyond the demands of the law. They have taken the pain out of sport as well. Eton has expelled violence from the Field Game. The ram, an elaborate bodily charge, has been banned after 150 years of continuous usage. Master-in-charge, Mike Grenier, insists that this curious manœuvre is now *"outmoded"*. Its absence, he argues, has made for *"a more enjoyable experience"* for the boys.[190] Clearly no future Waterloos are envisaged as a result. More to the point, nor is anything else. The demoralized has also become emasculated.

Moreover, these two developments are connected. They are the indirect products – in amateur games – of the professionalization of sports during the second half of the twentieth century; and the direct consequence – in both – of the still more recent rise of a related bogus expertise: sports science. Together, these malevolent modern departures have rendered the life and work of Bowen irrelevant; the world of Peel simply inconceivable. And their victims extend far beyond the ranks of a few over-protected public schoolboys. Today, they encompass all those – now nearly a majority of the population – who engage in a little or no voluntary physical activity but who have come to know all too well the torture of corporate-sponsored "team-building" games. How?

Amateurism – games for their own sake

To begin with professionalism, or rather, with its opposite. Amateurism does not just mean doing something "for the love", ie, without being paid. It does not even, necessarily, exclude all forms of payment.[191] It properly means doing something as an end in itself: generally regarded the best, indeed the only true reason for doing anything worthwhile. This involves playing cricket, for instance, just for the sake of playing cricket. Conceived analytically, that means that it presumes no distinction between the production and the consumption of cricket. Yet, precisely because it *is* an end, it need not be a narrowly conceived activity. It can be complex, various and subtle. Cricket is. It can require high skills, demand energetic effort and involve real danger. Cricket does. It can set intricate rules and presume age-old conventions. Think of cricket again. It can – it should – be an activity freely chosen, in the words of Lincoln Allison, *"in order to enrich experience"*.[192] In that way it can, and indeed it often does become a little world in itself; at once entirely self-sufficient and yet also acting as commentary upon and an addition to ordinary, mundane, existence. Some have even suggested that so conceived, it may point to a world beyond this world. Thus, Lord Mancroft:

> *Cricket [is] a game which the English, not being a spiritual people, have invented in order to give themselves some conception of eternity.*[193]

It goes without saying that anyone who really did equate cricket – or any other sport – with the eternal would be guilty, or at least might be guilty, of a certain narrowness of mind. But that sporting activity, sufficiently various and complex and yet wholly or largely uncoerced by social and economic necessity can be a mirror on life has long been understood. Few have put this better than P G Wodehouse:

> *Golf is…the infallible test. The man who can go into a patch of rough alone, with the knowledge that only God is watching him, and play his ball wherever it lies, is a man who will serve you faithfully and well.*[194]

To be sure, only a fool would take it as a true mirror, that is, a complete picture. But much of the enjoyment of life can be found in intelligent appreciation of its benevolent approximation to that image. Again, this is not to suggest that games are, or should be, solely gentle, peaceful and kind. On the contrary they can and should be by turn vigorous, aggressive and even unforgiving. As Jimmy Greaves, the great English footballer, once observed:

> *The thing about sport, any sport, is that swearing is very much part of it.*[195]

No doubt. But such sport was invariably fairer, safer, and to that degree more satisfying than real life. As such, it demonstrated the good in a way that elevated the stronger without breaking the weaker soul. No-one understood this better than Surtees:

> *'Unting is [whats] worth living for – the sport of kings, the image of war without its guilt, and only five-and-twenty per cent of the danger.*[196]

And that experience can still – just – be had. Consider the observation of Roger Scruton:

> *My life divides into three parts. In the first I was wretched; in the second ill at ease; in the third hunting.*[197]

But he does not hunt all the time; nor for his livelihood. He does not even hunt, by his own account, especially well.

The consequences of professionalism in sports and games are both good and bad. We should not entirely despise the good. They have raised the technical achievements of sport. They have furnished a standard of living to many which would otherwise have been denied them. Their achievements have, in turn, given pleasure to many more who have observed and, on occasion, tried to emulate them. But these are still inadequate justifications of professionalism. The same could also be said for prostitution or the sex industry more widely. Put another way: the professionalization of each and every aspect of life needs to be altogether more broadly argued for. And it is by no means obvious that rational men will conclude that it is always a good thing, in all circumstances.

Professionalism – single-minded pursuit of winning – the game only a means

Professionalism has one *inevitable* consequence. It separates production from consumption. For sports and games that means a distinction of erstwhile undifferentiated "players" into paid performers and paying spectators. This is not to say that no-one ever paid to watch amateur sport. Self-evidently, they did; in Rugby Union as recently as 1995. It is merely to observe that unambiguous change of emphasis which professionalization produces in the producer. Sensitive observers of Rugby Union will recognise this phenomenon well; all the more so for it being very recent.

The professional has a livelihood at stake. This makes him behave quite differently from the amateur. It makes him simultaneously more single-minded and more cautious than the amateur. He is more single-minded in pursuit of visible, measurable success in the trade that he plies. He is also more cautious in seeking to extend his career, at least to the extent that his sporting career represents the most efficient use of his talents, for as long as possible. This, in turn, has significant consequences for the game that he plays; eventually, at all levels of that game. Single-mindedness, of course, makes for technical improvement. In effect, it brings the mechanism of the division of labour to leisure. Just as in pin-making, this has obviously beneficial consequences. But as Adam Smith feared for the broader impact of repetitive activity upon the soul of the labourer, so any intelligent observer – not just this amateur sentimentalist – may reasonably note the effect of the single-minded pursuit of sport on an individual human being.[198] Many professional sportsmen themselves have honestly recognized as much. Consider the observations of Ian Botham:

To be no 1 in sport you have to have a narrow, tunnel, vision. [C]all it selfishness [or] arrogance, it's dog eat dog [with] no prisoners taken and none expected.[199]

Two consequences follow from this fact. Sport often ceases to be enjoyable for the sportsmen actually playing it. Once asked if he *enjoyed* playing professional football, Jack Charlton, a professional of some twenty years standing, responded:

Very occasionally. When you're four-nil up with ten minutes to go. Otherwise, honestly, no.[200]

For him, as no doubt for many others, playing the game had become wholly a means; no doubt to perfectly honourable purposes – providing for his family – but no longer an end in itself.

Co-operation between sportsmen becomes strictly instrumental

Secondly, co-operation between sportsmen becomes wholly instrumental. It is not that they do not co-operate; either with their own team-mates or even with the opposition. Of course they do. But, as professionals, they must have compelling reasons for such co-operation. And these need to be specific; certainly more specific than the end of the game itself. This is especially true of opponents. And it can take some extreme forms. Opponents of the notoriously aggressive West Indian fast-bowler of the 1970s and 1980s, Colin Croft, noted how he seemed *"full of hatred"*; a man who if he hit you would check *"just to make sure you* weren't *all right"*. Croft's honest response was that he viewed his opponents as obstacles to a better life for himself. Coming from as poor a background as he did, he could scarcely be expected to like them.[201]

More usually, instrumental co-operation between opponents puts a premium on honesty in their relations. This breaks down in the form of cheating. That can be a matter of deliberately not obeying the rules. The "professional foul" in football takes this form. That is, it is an example of deliberately and unfairly preventing an opponent from taking a legitimate advantage on the basis of his own skill or luck. The point is that it is effectively beyond retribution. Even the punishment of instant dismissal is insufficient provided the *sole* criterion of action is to win (or not to lose) the game. This is why professional footballers are now increasingly willing to risk stiff punishment either by cynically fouling their opponents (to prevent defeat) or equally cynically pretending to have been fouled (usually in the form of the strikers' "dive") to facilitate victory (usually by the award of an undeserved penalty). Techniques of cheating have, in effect, become part of the recognized skills-set of the modern professional sportsman.

The emergence of cheating

There are other forms of cheating too. These are usually concerned with undiscovered, unacknowledged, and unpunished default; batsmen who do not "walk" in cricket whilst knowing that they have in fact hit the ball; tennis players who do not concede a point even when the ball has struck their bodies. Those, deliberate and calculated, omissions amount to nothing less than a degradation of honour. They have lead to the "development", now endemic both in cricket and tennis, of technologically sophisticated arbitration apparatus quite specifically designed in order to remove the once presumed necessity of honour. Thus virtue is no longer honoured even in the breach. In effect, the dynamic of modern sport – how it is played and how it is regulated – has leeched the moral order out of sport. As one contemporary professional put it:

> *The rules in professional football are that sometimes you do everything to win the game.*[202]

Note his use of the word "rules".

More subtly still, professional sportsmen can only co-operate to a certain degree with their own team-mates. Stars earn more money than journeymen. Every place in a team is coveted by another. Victory nurtures collective team spirit. Defeat – the more common experience – necessitates more than a little protection of individual backs. Hence Geoffrey Boycott's observation, made during the tour of the West Indies of 1980-1 when continually confronted by what must have been the most ferocious fast-bowling quartet ever assembled. Under the brutal assault of Roberts, Holding, Gower and Croft, he eventually mused:

I wish I could paint my face black and go out and face our bowlers[203]

Most of these developments are of surprisingly recent origin. Few would date them further back than the late 1960s. Thus Danny Blanchflower, a great footballer of the 1950s, could still, in clear conscience, insist that:

The game is not first and last about winning. The game is about glory...doing things in style and with a flourish.[204]

No-one would honestly say that now; and not just about football. For what was once a *formally* professional game effectively yielded little in the way of material rewards as late as 1961. Other games remained only partially – and partisanly – professionalized during the same period; most obviously rugby. Thorough-going professionalization, and with it the effective exclusion of the amateur dimension, came late in most sports: cricket, from 1962; tennis since 1967; athletics as recently as 1983. Pervasive professionalization, in turn, facilitated commercialisation, or the effective integration of the world's major games into the entertainment industry. This is a product of only the last 20 years. Date it to the Los Angeles Olympics of 1984 if you wish.[205]

Without question, commercialisation has changed professional sport mightily. At its most basic, it has transformed some of the lowliest paid professions into strikingly effective mechanisms for the valorization of human capital. Twenty-five years ago, Matthew Fosh, a most promising young batsman at Essex, made a rational decision to abort a fledgling cricket career for the more securely lucrative pastures of the City. He would face an altogether more delicate calculation today. Just extend the time frame a little and the comparison becomes all the more poignant. Tommy Lawton, perhaps the finest of all English strikers before the War, ended life as a petty thief. David Beckham has become a multi-millionaire whilst still playing. And this is to say nothing of tennis and golf professionals.

The triumph of expertise in sport

At its most complex, commercialisation has changed the nature of what these sportsmen actually do. The more brazen aspects of commercialisation are, of course, just risible: tennis players as advertising hoardings, golfers as clothes horses. But, the more significant are less obvious and subtly more far-reaching. And they are grounded within the professional dynamic itself. Contemporary commercialisation has only made them worse. They can be understood as the results of the triumph of expertise in sport: of new technologies, of supposedly innovative techniques and, worst of all, of the whole gamut of sports science. These have been the instruments which have finally and decisively degraded the once noble amateur form of games; effectively expelling the intuitive wisdom which it contained, to leave an empty husk, appropriate only for the cultivation of physical fitness and mental gymnastics.

Let us be clear. Expertise always had its place in amateur games. No-one who reads Prince Ranjitsinghi's *Jubilee Book of Cricket* will doubt that the late-Victorian cricketer took the science of his sport very seriously indeed.[206] But they also acknowledged the implicit tension between developmental science and timeless honour in sports. That is why the Edwardians could debate in all seriousness whether or not the "googly" (the off-spin delivery bowled with a leg-break action) was or was not cricket: if skill then cricket, if deception then not. They determined, in the end, for skill.[207] This was not hypocritical. It was agonised. The whole purpose of modern sports science is not merely to render such questions ridiculous. It is to redefine sporting activity in such a way as to ensure that they could never even be asked. It does this by reducing sport to *pure* technique; in effect, to a complex set of means. No end, apart from victory, is envisaged. More to the point: no end, apart from victory, could under its auspices ever even possibly be envisaged.

This is most clearly the case in the matter of technology. Here, expertise is devoted not simply to victory but to uncomplicated, decisive and preferably swift victory. To be sure both sides usually have access to the same technology. Thus, technological development can rarely be stigmatised as unfair and is, accordingly, still more rarely proscribed; especially in professional sport.[208] But its transformative impact on the affected games is invariably enormous. And it has never been with the effect of *increasing* the subtlety, balance and moral order of those activities. Think of the impact of steel-framed tennis rackets on the men's game in particular. Moreover, the women's game is catching up fast. Venus Williams commonly serves faster than Rod Laver ever did.

None of this makes sport any easier. But it does make it still more physical. And that puts a premium not just on fitness but also upon physique: think of the Williams sisters more generally. Moreover, it places a new emphasis not simply on what can be given, physically, but on what has been attained: think of the Williams sisters again. At its most sinister, that means body-transforming drugs, ineffectively banned in most sports. At its most commonplace, it involves strict dietary and other physical regimes, now universally pursued in every sport. The desired effect – no less than the end in sight – is to transform sportsmen and women into machines with which to play games. Increasingly, the result is something all too distressingly like the envisaged image. Think of the Williams sisters one last time.

So ambitious a project is rarely within the capacity of one sportsman or woman, however dedicated. Perhaps the last truly self-sufficient professional in this respect was Boycott himself; and he retired in 1986.[209] The norm today is the professionally-trained and multiply-prepared public performer: the sportsman or woman with accompanying pharmacist and physician, dietician and psychologist, now even hypnotist; all invariably in tow and all on the payroll. Sportsmen and women of this type – and they are increasingly common – have not just ceased to be the lowly-paid employees of "yesteryear". They have become major employers in their own right. And what they hire are specific, skilled services. Their relations with those who provide services are necessarily professional; that is, instrumental and amoral.

In this world, the very idea of one man and his conscience has become a literal nonsense. The professional development of far too many people is at stake. To take only the most extreme example: when the penalty kick was introduced into professional football, the Corinthian Casuals, a predominantly public school and amateur club, announced a policy of refusing to score from so low a device. Today, with millions of pounds at stake in penalty "shoot-outs" designed to separate teams at the end of gruelling tournaments, professional footballers are routinely prepared in "stress-management" techniques in order to cope with the scale of the tasks involved: this in addition to being coached on how best to take the penalty itself.[210]

Amateur games in terminal decline

This is more than a matter for nostalgia, for it points to a profound social change. This is encapsulated by the contemporary eclipse of organized games in this country. To be sure, *professional* sport thrives as never before. So do professional sportsmen and women; and, increasingly those with related professional services to sell. But organized, amateur, sport is in terminal decline. There are many reasons for this. To some extent, it is the inevitable product of the decline of voluntary, associated, life more generally.[211] But only to some extent; more significantly, it is the result of an altogether more specific re-evaluation of the wider benefits of organized sport in contemporary society; and a belittling re-evaluation at that. Put bluntly: now teaching nothing broad or good, sport finds fewer and fewer public benefactors and supporters.

Forget the *Sports Council* or *Sports England*. Local authorities and schools are now selling off their playing fields as fast as the law will allow them. Perhaps 5,000 went this way nationally between 1981 and 1997. Most informed observers expect around another 1,000 such applications in 2002. And that under a government formally pledged to *reverse* the trend.[212] Naturally, these developments provoke periodic protest. But the force of public objection is weak. Sport and games have a low municipal profile. And it is difficult to argue why, in their modern form, they *should* be treated otherwise. Sport and games play no significant part in the national curriculum. Ditto. Cash-starved executives can scarcely be condemned for seeking to realize potentially valuable assets. What they currently administer are huge liabilities. So they try to avoid them. The acknowledged trick is to close them, thereby proving they are unwanted; and then to sell them.[213] What of public health and well-being? That has become an argument for the gym. It occupies less space; ie, it is cheaper. It permits sufficient exercise in a shorter period of time; thus, it is more efficient. It requires no-one to organize anything. It does not even require anyone to talk to anyone else. No wonder it is prospering in our time. Finally, it is safer. And what is the point of exercise for health unless it is wholly safe?

The business training game – the ultimate degradation

Naturally, it need not be entirely pointless. And a new kind of game is very pointed indeed. This is the game that no-one actually wants to play. That is why it is only played at work. It is the "training game". It represents the ultimate perversion of games which "professional" and expertise – together – have wrought. In this context, the professional and expert is the facilitator. He or she differs from the coach or even presumed personal trainer in being (at least initially) the *only* person who actually knows the end of the game. All the other players are means. Put another way: they are coerced. His or her "expertise" takes the form of so manipulating their (coerced) actions as to bring about a measurable degree of personal or collective development in them. To whose benefit? The objects of such experiments are invariably the employees of larger, bureaucratic organizations. The subjects (ie, those who pay for them) are usually their employers. As such, these games are expected to produce managerially defined results. After a fashion, they do.

This does not prevent the games themselves from being banal. On the contrary, the more banal invariably the better. A standard civil service so-called "energizer" involves collecting together a small group of people and then:

a) Inflating as many balloons as possible *or*
b) Relay activities racing balloons pushed with breath *or even*
c) Relay activity moving a balloon wedged between two people.

This is followed by "introduction activity" in which all partners have to keep their balloons in the air at the same time, possibly including an exchange of balloons. The point of all this is to break down the inhibitions of so-called "completers"; members of a team who are otherwise "never at ease until they have personally checked every detail and made sure everything has been done". These "morale-lowering worriers" will "apparently depress everyone else", unless reformed. However, subject to training, their "relentless follow-through" can become "a real asset".[214]

Now compare the world of Bowen with Marlene Caroselli's *Great Session Openers, Closers and Energizers: Quick Activities for Warming Up Your Audience and Ending on a High Note.*[215] He was an educator. She is a "professional trainer". He was a mere MA. She has a doctorate from the University of Rochester. He extolled the inherent virtues of traditional sports. She makes up her own games and activities. His common pursuits obeyed common rules. She invents the rules of her preferred activities as she goes along. He joined in with the boys. She counsels other facilitators only. He strove for mutual respect. She demands of her charges their commitment to "*a constant upgrading of your professional repertoire*".[216] And how are they to achieve this? By submitting to more unknown and unknowable games, played according to hidden instructions and organized by rank; all their lives.

Some have doubted the efficacy, and even propriety, of the so-called Victorian "cult of athleticism". But their games were never as sinister as this.

CHAPTER 7

Appreciating the arts

Athena S Leoussi

The decline of art is part of the decline of wisdom

The decline of art in the hands of some of the most prominent of modern artists is not a novel observation. It is, however, worth reiterating – at every opportunity. First, because of the importance of the artistic interest in human life; and, second, because much of the malaise of contemporary art belongs to an unease in the whole of our contemporary culture: the conflict between wisdom and expertise, depth and surface. In its partiality to wisdom, to the primacy of good judgment in all spheres of conduct, this essay argues for more time and less haste: for time to learn and to think, and then to create. It argues, firstly, for the necessity for modern artists to consider their work as an integral part of a long and great artistic tradition; and secondly, to recognize their duty to create culture. This duty consists in the distinctive obligation of artists, towards both art collectors and the viewing public, to cultivate and satisfy, through their work, the sense of beauty.

The appreciation of art is the appreciation of beauty

Every work of art must announce itself as such, which can only be done by what we call sensual beauty or grace.[217]

"Who still thinks that painting aims at beauty?" the late art historian, Sir Ernst Gombrich, enquired upon his acceptance of the Goethe Prize of the city of Frankfurt in September 1994.[218] For much of modern art has rejected, both in theory and in practice, the quest for beauty, submerging the aesthetic interest which art seeks to satisfy.

The artistic interest, as Walter Pater most movingly observed, is "native in the human soul".[219] It is present in the Hebrew Bible, even though the Second Commandment prohibited plastic art in Israel, banishing all images as "vile". We find it, for example, in *Exodus*, chapter 28, defined as beauty:

> *And thou shalt make holy garments for Aaron thy brother for glory and for beauty;*

and in chapter 36 as craftsmanship, in the making of the tabernacle. The tabernacle was made by men

> *in whom the Lord put wisdom and understanding to know how to work all manner of work for the service of the sanctuary.*

And they made curtains of "fine twined linen, and blue, and purple, and scarlet", with cherubim of "cunning work".

But while the suppression of the beautiful in contemporary art has not passed unnoticed, it has not been rectified. That suppression can only bring frustration, and the search for fulfilment away from the ugliness of modern art. Beauty is a god in exile. We find it more often in descriptions of mathematical equations than in accounts of modern works of art. The concern for "tricks", for "fun", for the unusual and for the shocking, the subversive and the sensational characterizes much of modern art. This is evident in the most controversial of modern British art institutions, the Turner Prize, and in the work of such recipients as Damien Hirst (1995), Chris Ofili (1998), and Martin Creed (2001).

When considering the work of these artists, one must abandon all hope, as Dante said at the gates of hell. One will search in vain for release in modern art: for the aesthetic dimension in art, or for any attempt to elevate or gladden the spirit. Such desires were still moving the brush of a number of modern artists, well into the twentieth century, of whom Matisse is the most typical. For him, art should be like a comfortable armchair:

> *What I dream of is an art of balance, of purity and serenity devoid of troubling or depressing subject matter...a soothing, calming influence*

on the mind, rather like a good armchair which provides relaxation from physical fatigue. [220]

The isolation of the aesthetic feeling from all other kinds of feeling was an achievement in the long yearning of mankind for self-knowledge. In its fullest realization it can be dated with precision to the second half of the eighteenth century, in Germany, in the writings of Johann Joachim Winckelmann and Immanuel Kant. Kant identified the capacity of the human mind to apprehend beauty as, in truth, an existential imperative. Winckelmann claimed to have located its supreme object, cause and stimulus, in the *edel Einfalt und stille Grösse,* the noble simplicity and calm grandeur, of classical art.

Winckelmann's idea, that beauty is like the purest water, that the less taste it has the better it is, took root in European culture to inspire a belief in art for art's sake, so that each work of art might appear to the eye like an ornament. The work of Dominique Ingres, whose love of the female form gave rise to the most sensual and at the same time most abstract designs of Western art, came to be seen as the first embodiment of the new creed.

Tradition is a set of solutions which frees the creativity of each generation by enabling it

Tradition is not the dead hand of the past but rather the hand of the gardener, which nourishes and elicits tendencies of judgment which would otherwise not be strong enough to emerge on their own. In this respect tradition is an encouragement to incipient individuality rather than its enemy. It is a stimulant…rather than an opiate. [221]

The classical ideal was subject to strict canons, but Winckelmann knew that these rules were the self-imposed laws of free men. They were the outcome of Greek freedom, *Freiheit:*

Through freedom the thinking of the entire people rose up like a noble branch from a healthy trunk. [222]

The classical rules of proportion were not meant to enslave, but to liberate. They gave Greek artists the freedom which comes with every solution. The problem of Greek artists was how to represent the beauty of the human body. However, under the influence of fanatics and sterile thinkers, the Greek solution, as embodied in Greek art, became an imposition. It was deprived of the flexibility and suggestiveness which characterizes a fully absorbed tradition.[223] The German love of Greece became unlike true love, a mingling of souls, but an enslavement of one soul to another: the mechanical imitation of set models. The tyranny of Greece over Germany transformed Greek statuary into Ezekiel's vision, a valley of dry bones. It gave tradition, man's relation to his past, a bad name.

Nevertheless, Winckelmann's classicism, his advocacy of the imitation of Greece in painting and sculpture, liberated the aesthetic impulse as an end in itself. The idea of beauty suffused Western culture, freeing art from subjection to moral content. In England, the desire for beauty was most memorably expressed in Matthew Arnold's notion of "sweetness". As an injunction about how to live our lives, sweetness had to be combined, to Arnold's mind, and in a rather Kantian fashion, with the light of reason, and with Judaeo-Christian ethics. Still, the aesthetic life had been recognized for what it was: as both a human and a cultural impulse.

Formalism has limited the aesthetic value of art

For a long time the new awakening to pure beauty, the new realization, previously only dimly felt, that the shapes and colours of this world should be sources of infinite pleasure, and that they should be the subject-matter of art, was a gain. The belief in what came to be referred to as "the autonomy of art", intensified sensitivity to technique, to craftsmanship and, in general, to the formal qualities of works of art. However, by the middle of the twentieth century, the cultivation of the autonomy of art had resulted in its impoverishment. This was due, first, to the apprehension of both the world and of art as pure form, as the drawing of diagonals and the analysis of pyramids.[224] This formalism came to be pursued at the expense of subject-matter. The representation of the external world eventually dissolved it into its simplest, and most minimal, formal properties. Art lost its references to the natural and moral worlds, beyond recognition. It became abstract.

A second excess of the cult of the autonomy of art was the negation of beauty in its essential province, the sphere of artistic creation. Not unrelated to the first, it made artists, on the one hand indifferent, if not averse, to creating beauty, and, on the other, ultimately blind to the beauties of the natural world. This came about with the final triumph of means over ends: the preoccupation with materials. The increasing interest in the peculiar properties of materials, in their capacity to bend, to rust, to expand, to absorb or repel pigment, has led artists and their public, to adopt the motives of the engineer. Anish Kapoor's art is one of the few exceptions, along with that of Rachel Whiteread.

It may thus be said that the recognition of the aesthetic feeling had some unintended and unwanted consequences for Western art. Not so much the isolation of this feeling from all other kinds of feeling associated with the subject-matter of art, but rather, and most importantly, the re-orientation of art towards abstraction. This led, inadvertently, to the very submergence of the aesthetic feeling which had made abstraction both possible and, in its early stages, acceptable, as the purest consummation of this feeling. The works of Mark Rothko and Howard Hodgkin can only serve as evidence of how much talent, skill and sensitivity is required for success with abstraction.

If the separation of the aesthetic life from our other lives should be artificial, then it could be argued that there is a link between sweetness and civility in man. If the wholeness of human existence should be upheld, in Kantian fashion, in which the true, the good and the beautiful must be combined, in one way or another, then this affinity of feelings should not be allowed to be broken. Rather, it should be pursued, at least as a cultural ideal, not only against the assaults of modern art, but also against the Nazi form of love of art, and other such instances of cultural disjunction. Nowhere has this affinity been expressed more sweetly than in Shakespeare's observations on the meaning of the love of sweetness in music, in *The Merchant of Venice:*

The man that hath no music in himself,
Nor is not mov'd with concord of sweet sounds,
Is fit for treasons, stratagems, and spoils;
The motions of his spirit are dull as night,
And his affections dark as Erebus.
Let no such man be trusted.

While the memorable opening lines of *Twelfth Night* suggest the very influence which sweetness may have on the soul, to impel it to love more:

If music be the food of love, play on,
Give me excess of it....

All great art embodies the human impulse to live

L'art est un anti-destin (Art is a revolt against fate).[225]

It has been admitted since time immemorial, that, as Victor Hugo put it, *"Nous sommes tous condamnés à mort"*. Malraux's observation, that art is a revolt against fate, may be understood in this context. True works of art are eternal creations. They continue to live after the death of their creator, extending his life, not simply as a memory but as an offspring. The Hippocratic slogan, better known in its Latin version, *ars longa vita brevis*, is a consoling thought at the edge of the abyss.

And long life is not just the happy destiny of great art, but also the ambition of great artists: to express and leave behind, for everyone to see, the most inspiring notions which captured their spirit; to immortalize those moments of heightened awareness to which, as individuals, they gave form and colour. To make the absent present, in more than one sense of the word; to crystallize and to preserve what is worth preserving in the span of human understanding and expression, is the aim of art. Indeed, great art achieves more than mere survival, for it is both an act of self-affirmation, and an act of fellowship – an offering to others of something beneficial to them. Art expresses the desire that the work of man should give joy to man. It is thus, at one and the same time, both inwardly and outwardly directed.

Much of what is considered best in modern art is self-obsessed, precarious and "nowish" – and is meant to be so. It is not worth keeping, nor, indeed, transmitting. For, to use Kurt Schwitters' terminology for his own art, it is *Merzbild*, by which he meant rubbish; and *Nichtkunst*, not art. It idealizes the discarded and the excreted. It is "Dada". More recent examples are Chris Ofili's elephant dung paintings and Tracey Emin's proud display of her soiled underwear and sheets, in "My Bed".

Over-exposure to modern art is dangerous; it degrades and demoralizes its viewers, leading them to forget that art is one of the pleasures and consolations of life. Together with religion, learning and love, art gives meaning and justification to human existence. Man's ability to create culture, ideals by which to live and strive for, has been denied by modern art with its nihilism, destructiveness and refusal to make distinctions – to separate the sacred from the profane; the beautiful from the ugly, and, ultimately, good from evil. If art is creation, then it should be a life-giving force, like the Biblical creation.

Artistic creation is enriched by the achievements of past art

After indulging early in the wild
Demonic-genius cult of boisterous youth
You later slowly searched for higher truth
By turning to the wise divinely-mild.[226]

The dissociation of art from tradition, from the history of artistic creation, is a dominant feature of modern art education and practice. Like a modern Athene, the contemporary artist claims to have been born in full armour; or, that he or she is entitled to re-invent their craft *ex nihilo*, with "freshness and originality" (Herbert Read). But even the most rebellious of nineteenth-century French artists, the Impressionists, those very artists who created both the conditions and the idea of a modern art, were soon to regret their contempt for "*l'art des musées*". For they discovered, early enough, that over-reliance on one's own "*petite sensation*" was incapacitating: they could neither draw, nor paint. The conscious obliteration of all artistic learning, the dogmatic un-learning of technique and craftsmanship which they had advocated, was a "blind alley". And they returned to the museums – to Rome and the Louvre. Through the return to the old shrines of art, and through the imaginative fusion of the old with the new, Impressionism acquired a new solidity and structure, becoming itself an art worthy of a museum.

The experience has since been repeated many times. Yet, much of modern art training instructs students to look and draw, as if drawing were a purely sensory activity, requiring no hands, no learning of the conventions of drawing – no education. This attitude to art education which rejects the very idea and practice of education is widely spread on both sides of the Atlantic, as is shown in an excellent article by Catesby Leigh, in the January/February 2002 issue of *The American*

Enterprise. Leigh points out that the modernist view tells art students that if they can see, they can draw. In contrast, the traditionalist view tells art students that they do not have to make up conventions: "that the best way to learn to draw a horse is to copy good drawings of horses".[227]

Artistic value depends not on the capacity of art to subvert tradition, but on its capacity to perpetuate past achievements and expand them

The dissociation of modern art from its own history is denial of the very conditions of its existence as an established, respected and publicly-sponsored component of Western life. In the Frankfurt speech mentioned earlier, Gombrich had remarked on "that great watershed" which divides the world of Goethe from our own world. Although he had entitled his speech, "Goethe: the Mediator of Classical Values", he emphasized that Goethe's world, in its artistic concerns, had sought nourishment, not only in classical art, but also in the whole of art; for this tradition is a source of life, with subjects, materials, and techniques, all contributing solutions to artistic problems.

> *Goethe had the right to feel at home everywhere. In the England of Shakespeare and Byron no less than in the France of Diderot and in the Italy of Benvenuto Cellini and Tasso; indeed in the Persia of Hafiz, and the India of Kalidasa, from whose Sanskrit play Sakuntala Goethe took the idea of a Prelude on the Stage for his Faust.*[228]

All too often, the modern world has denied its rich inheritance, rejecting all received ideas, and refusing to look back for fear that it might be petrified. It has established the forward look as the best attitude to life. But except for the gifted few, the resulting vista is a desert, empty of forms. Modernism is founded on the belief in the authority of the future and the rejection of the past. This state of mind can only be sustained by negative means: by a continuous loss of memory, and the perpetual severing of the spiritual umbilical cord which binds one generation to another. Nor has the rejection of traditional values and techniques benefited gifted artists, for those endowed with the rare ability to represent our world with their hands, with colour, paint or marble, have squandered their gift misled by abstraction. Willem de Kooning is one of these great, but lost souls of modern art – a genius *manqué*.

Emotionally, modernism can be seen as a condition of arrested adolescence: of perpetual revolt against the father and predecessors, and an uncompromising affirmation of the self. With roots in the Romantic age, it is a tradition which denies tradition. It is also a distortion of the aims of Romanticism, in which rejection of authority only meant universal inclusion, a humanism which embraced everything which gave pleasure in the past. It meant, as Walter Pater observed, that nothing which had actually interested men and women should ever lose its vitality. And this concern to preserve the vitality of the past in the present, this acceptance of the knowledge and wisdom of the ages which we call tradition, is what constitutes the culture of every human society. It is this culture which creates a human being. For the human being, as Émile Durkheim observed, is not so much a point of departure, as a point of arrival. To wipe the slate clean in art, as indeed, in any other sphere of human endeavour, is to remove the very conditions, not only of art's existence, but also of one's originality.

The condition of modern art is a moral condition. Many modern artists do not have the humility and wisdom to learn from their predecessors. They also lack the courage, patience and diligence to place themselves in this long and continuous line of invention and delight which constitutes past art. Misled by their teachers, they refuse to engage with this inheritance, to take from it, to be enriched by it, and to expand it.

As already noted, Goethe embraced culture, *Bildung*.[229] And if, in late eighteenth- and nineteenth-century Germany, *Bildung* came to mean, pre-eminently, the classical tradition, this was not, and is not now, the only tradition in Western, or world culture. Furthermore, all traditions encompass a variety of human creations. Indeed, the history of Western art is one of constant change and revival: a series of reactions and solutions to inherited problems, followed by the consideration of new. And these changes were not all-embracing; neither did they occur in a vacuum, but rather from a consideration of this or that aspect of what had gone before. This is the case with Greek, Byzantine, Gothic and Renaissance art, Rococo, Neo-Classicism, Impressionism, Expressionism, Cubism, and at last abstract art, which ended the dialogue with the past. This uprooting made art narrow, un-self-critical and self-indulgent.

An anti-cultural art is anti-human

Modern art is anti-human in two senses: first, in its lack of appreciation of the expectations of its public; their ideas, and their values, what they know and what they aspire towards. Although art is a communicative activity, much modern art conveys nothing and shares nothing with its public. The following passage may serve to illustrate the effect which true art has on its public, namely, the sense of human accomplishment:

> *We visited Borgo San Sepolcro, a small place in those days quite difficult to get at, situated, as I recall, in the heart of Umbria. In a bleak room of its town hall one was suddenly face to face with the Resurrection, the masterpiece of Piero della Francesca...We ate our spaghetti that morning with a sense of high achievement, for who can see a great picture or read a great book without taking some of the credit for it himself?*[230]

And second, modern art has little interest in the human form. Frank Auerbach, Francis Bacon, David Hockney and Lucian Freud, are exceptional among contemporary artists. The human basis of art is a vital part of the Western humanistic heritage, from Greece through to the Italian Renaissance and early modernism. It is evident in the ancient legend that, as Lessing put it, "Love prompted the first attempt in the plastic arts"[231]: the desire to capture the beloved. Modern art has rejected the careful study of the human form in favour of arbitrary and incomprehensible arrangements, or "installations" of materials.

Modern art addresses the expert rather than the community

If modern art does manage to have a constituency of support, this consists predominantly of other artists, art experts and misguided collectors and youths. A visit to the two Tate Galleries, in London, may serve as an index to the kind of appreciation which modern art receives. Tate Modern tends to resemble night in Leicester Square: full of young people expecting to be entertained, to have fun, with images of dangling genitalia and other such types of extreme subject-matter with which contemporary artists try to gain attention. Tate Britain is almost empty of youth, except for school groups: it requires a different mood. Its art encompasses and crystallizes the richness, not only of British, but also of universal experience, through its references to literature, politics, philosophical ideas, the pursuit of love, and the sense of beauty. It is serious, calling for a response from the mind and the emotions.

It is interesting, in this context, to think of that great separatist of the Berlin Secession, the Norwegian Expressionist artist, Edvard Munch. Munch had advocated, at least for his own art, a very different attitude to that which we discern among contemporary artists: respect. In 1889 he wrote in his diary his views on art: "We should no longer paint interiors with people reading and women knitting. We should paint real people, who breathe, feel, suffer and love". Through this humanism, through this concern with the depiction of the interior life of man, Munch expected art to command the same respect as the old Christian religion:

People would respect the power, the sanctity of it and they would take off their hats as they do in a church.[232]

Modern art, especially of the most "advanced" and least tradition-bound type, aims to impress the art expert and entertain the young. But the experts are more important, for they are the key to the financial success of the modern artist. The experts are, of course, as much disconnected from their living culture as the artist, with whom they inhabit a mysterious world, speaking a mystical language. The modern art expert likes art only in so far as it communicates obscure formal ideas, such as "verticality" (Rosalind Krauss), or "the look of the void" (Clement Greenberg). Thus, the expert is clearly not, as one might expect, a mediator between the artist and the public, an informed and sensitive representative and guide of public taste. If there is some thought about the public, it is one of contempt.

Modern art experts also praise works of art when they are supposed to embody an "attitude", a "viewpoint". And the more socially "subversive" or "radical" the viewpoint is, the more it qualifies as art; so much so that the viewpoint becomes more important than hard-won technical skill. Andy Warhol's mass-produced images, as, indeed, his films, involved no skill on his part, of which, anyway, he had very little. He used studio assistants and real technical experts to realise his "viewpoint" – the idea of mechanical mass-production *as* art, an idea which debased art. How different has this idea been from the Victorian desire to make mechanically produced objects beautiful.

In its association with that other, and equally artless idea, that of the *objet trouvé*, the Viewpoint School of Art has deemed art by decree: art resides not in certain qualities of an object, but in its context. And the most decisive context, outside the modern art gallery, is the *will* that an object should constitute an art object, such as Marcel Duchamp's still greatly admired *pissoir* (urinal) of 1917. Here again, the belief that art is what the "artist", like the primordial Adam, calls "art", perpetuates some of the more negative aspects of the old Romantic relativism: its pessimism, nihilism and cult of the *will*. And since many art schools do not value either technical skill, or learning, but a *will*, the logical conclusion might well be that we are all artists!

Art should not be alienated from community

No one who regards the literature of the middle ages can fail to notice...its close association with the traditions and history (as then understood) of the society which rejoiced in it...The same is true of Greek literature. Both sprang from the life of the people and gave to that life its spiritual sanction, together with a sense of stability, by linking it up with the immemorial past.[233]

Ut pictura poesis: what applies to painting and sculpture, also applies to literature, and *vice versa*. Much of modern art in England shows little respect for English culture. It may even be said that it deliberately corrupts the English sensibility towards tradition and nature.[234] This may be explained, not only as a result of modernism, but also of the internationalisation, if not globalisation, of art. Art no longer addresses a particular, national culture, but rather an international *Gesellschaft* of artists, art experts and art collectors. The outlook of this network society is an eccentric sub-culture, detached from the centres of substantive cultural life. It is a culture untouched by life as it is actually lived, a Utopian culture which has evolved in the recesses of abundance and *ennui*. It is thus devoid of human understanding in which it has little interest. It tends to isolate and alienate the artist from genuine culture and community. But if art should be a cultural expression, and have a civilizing influence, then like Solon's laws, it must address and reinforce the customs and sentiments of a particular community. Solon made laws to fit men, while Lycurgus made men fit the laws. And if art should follow Solon's path and engage with real life, then it will also acquire universal significance.

By rejecting tradition, modern British artists compromise that great achievement of their predecessors: the restoration of the visual arts in Britain

...national qualities are far from permanent. There occur every now and then cultural changes, changes of heart and mind, which go so deep that they may bury certain qualities for ever or for a long time and beget new ones. In [English] art such a change is supposed to have taken place at the time of the Reformation, with the result that fine art went under for two hundred years. But, though both lack of demand for certain types of painting and sculpture and Protestantism as such certainly had their effects, the change actually began long before the Reformation...[T]he next major break in English cultural and aesthetic development happened only in the years between 1840 and 1860.[235]

Modern art in Britain has tried to obliterate the efforts of previous generations who, not so long ago, tried to cultivate in the British soul the sense of the outward beauty of things, not as a sin, which is how Protestantism had come to view it, but as a virtue. This effort can be said to have begun belatedly, as compared with similar developments in Catholic countries, in France, and, above all, in Renaissance Italy. It was only in the late eighteenth century that an academic tradition became established in England, with the foundation of the Royal Academy of Arts in 1768, and it was not until the middle of Queen Victoria's reign that a genuinely aesthetic movement, a blossoming of painting and sculpture, could flourish in Britain. And everywhere there was

an impression of surprise, as of people first waking from the golden age, at fire, snow, wine, the touch of water as one swims, the salt taste of the sea...[236]

Until that time, the true vehicles of the British sense of beauty had been literature and architecture. This great cultural achievement of

British artists, with all its manifold implications, must not be left unrecognized. Instead, it must inspire young artists to continue and expand the work of their predecessors, in an affirmation and appreciation of the visual arts.

Author's note:

I should like to thank Leo Bernard for his kind, wise and learned advice and comments. And, as always, David Marsland.

Helping those less fortunate than ourselves

Daniel Lapin

Giving charity is not as easy as it appears

Not everyone does it. Not even every decent person does it. But many people do act on the urge they feel to help those they perceive as less fortunate. The urge to ameliorate the plight of the poor seems to be so deeply embedded in the Western tradition that it easily became part of the political agenda of all those who wished to govern. To the extent that politics is nothing more than the practical application of deeply held values, Western populations informed their leaders of their willingness to devote some of their resources to helping others on a large scale. The result was tax-supported charity in most Western democracies.

However, the entire history of the post World War II Western welfare states suggests that this task is a lot harder than it might appear. In spite of unimaginably vast sums of money being lavished on this altruistic cause, all measurable statistics reveal little or no progress. Those whom state bureaucracies catalogue as poor still constitute as large, or as is the case in many countries, a larger part of the population as they did thirty years ago. Altogether, the task of helping people seems fraught with problems. For a start, helping others is often complicated by unintended consequences. Among these is that long lines tend to form in front of anyone handing out money. Instead of responding benevolently to a real need, charitable foundations often discover that hopeful beneficiaries frequently design a need to match the giving specifications of the donor. In this way, needs apparently expand to exploit the availability of help. State agencies have hardly been immune from this exploitation as the many notorious "welfare queen" cases suggest.

Unintended consequences of charity

Many other unintended consequences impair attempts to help. For instance, careless help often seems to breed long-term dependency which tragically undermines the original purpose. Assistance dispensed bureaucratically occasionally seems to produce a sense of entitlement and resentment among recipients. Generous assistance programs often get blamed for large-scale immigration, both legal and illegal. States invariably grow enormous bureaucratic juggernauts to administer the giving. Eventually more money goes to pay the salaries of those dispensing assistance than finds its way into the hands of the unfortunate. These, along with many other problems, fill phil-anthropists, private and public agencies, public policy experts, and governments with despair. In spite of countless studies, analyses, public policy conferences, and philanthropic roundtables, the problems still persist. Thirty years of scientifically designed programs and academic scrutiny still leave the landscape pretty much the way it might have appeared had no efforts ever been made. By any measure, those of us who had hoped to make major inroads on poverty have not gotten our money's worth. Have we been using the wrong tools for the job?

Learning from the past and peering into the future

Some things, like raising children, are best accomplished by consulting the past, others, like building anti-lock braking systems for motorcycles, by peering into the future. The past, for instance, has little to contribute in the search for a cure for cancer. The future is unlikely to shed any light on how best to civilize the human male's sexual obsessions. Technological development seems to emphasize how rapidly the world is changing, while at one and the same time it seems to camouflage how little things have really changed. Human greatness born of handed-down wisdom and experience still counts for something although we confuse it with technical proficiency. The latter could, in principle, be taught to a gorilla or programmed into a machine, while the former is unique to a human being. I recall once visiting a boatyard in the south of England that was still building the prettiest little sailing sloops out of fine English oak – and doing so entirely by hand. The time was rapidly passing for seeing boats being built, much as they used to be built, of wood by skilled craftsmen rather than of plastic by unskilled help. Fibreglass can be applied to the inside of a mould by machines or by relatively unskilled labour and then popped out as soon as it has hardened and cured. Boat hulls can be turned out rapidly and inexpensively because little skill is required. By contrast, the craftsmen at the Hilyard boatyard near Southampton had spent a lifetime building wooden boats by hand. Many of these men were the sons of those who had also spent their lives building exquisite yachts out of ancient oak forests.

I watched one older artisan planking what I remember to be about a thirty-foot boat. He had planked the side all the way down from the sheer, or deck line, and all the way up from the keel until all that remained was space for the last plank to be laid up against the frames. The gap was about thirty feet long from stem to stern. Its width varied between about six or seven inches in the middle to about one or two inches at each end. This was because the cross section of a sailing boat varies from narrow at bow and stern to a wine-glass appearance amidships. Since the same number of planks are used from deck to keel, and since the distance is obviously so much greater at the middle of the vessel than it is at either end, each plank must be far wider toward its middle than at either of its ends. I describe this process in some detail not because I think you will ever need to know, but because I want you to comprehend the enormity of the feat I am about to relate.

While I stood and watched, the wrinkled carpenter stepped back and, with some obvious satisfaction at being so close to finishing his project, gazed adoringly at the lovely ship. Eyeing the last remaining gap to be planked, he ambled over to the pile of fresh lumber and picked out a long slender plank that must have been about thirty-five feet long and about ten inches wide. After placing it in several vices set into a long workbench, he began planing down its edge to reduce its width. I waited to see him take some measurements off the hull but he never did. Every now and again he would glance over his shoulder and narrow his eyes as he stared at the gap in the planking, as if it offended him personally. It finally dawned on me that he was visually measuring his work against the gap into which it would have to fit perfectly. Not only was there the length and constantly varying width for him to contend with, but there was also a bevel that needed to be set into both the upper and lower edges of the new plank to later accept the caulking.

Swinging backward and forward, he planed away so much that his big old work boots were almost concealed by fresh, fragrant shavings. (I can smell them to this day.) The shavings fell from his hissing plane until he finally released the plank from the vice, lifted it to his shoulders, and carried it over to the boat where he offered it up to the gap. He clamped it into position, stepped back again and ambled the length of the boat without taking his eyes off his new plank. Then he took the plank back to the workbench, where he toiled at it for a while before returning it to the boat. It fitted perfectly. He glued and screwed it into place, quite oblivious to the fact that he had casually carried off a feat of sheer magic. I was incredibly moved as I realized that the world would soon cease to see anything like this again.

There was very little technology to see that afternoon at the Hilyard boatyard in south England. But no more than a hundred miles away, in a spanking-new factory belonging to Russell Marine, twenty new fibreglass boats had been built in moulds in less time than it took the Hilyard works to build just one wooden boat. They were going to be considerably less expensive and much easier to own and maintain.

Technology can make better products than craftsmanship

Which was the superior achievement? Using advanced technology, Russell Marine was churning out large numbers of identical plastic boats that sold for reasonable sums of money and, for the first time ever, brought leisure boating to England's ordinary citizens. Russell Marine was also on its way to becoming a successful company that earned outstanding returns for its shareholders by using every latest advance in manufacturing technology. The Hilyard yard represented a dying industry. Wooden boat building of that kind no longer exists. They were producing works of art for connoisseurs. Their boats were expensive and difficult to maintain, but they were beautiful, hand-crafted creations. Which was superior?

I do not think there is much doubt that in spite of our nostalgia for Hilyard, the shiny new factory was doing the better job from an economic perspective. The proof was that they remained in business whereas the Hilyard enterprise finally closed. They were pleasing more people. Yet, in spite of all this, we must constantly remain aware that the plastic factory never did and never will produce outstanding craftsmen. Their technology allows them to succeed in spite of the fact that their best employee has none of the skills, quality, or character strength of Hilyard's youngest apprentice.

But not better people

Though undoubtedly marvellous, technology has the capacity to conceal a decline in the human qualities of people. One dull child with a twelve-dollar calculator can outshine a brilliant nineteenth-century accountant doing mental arithmetic. The juvenile's accuracy and speed will eclipse that of the man who held the finances of large corporations in his head just one hundred years ago. Let us not fall into the trap of considering the adolescent superior to last generation's accountant. His performance may be superior, but as a person, he is not as fully developed. Faced with the choice, we might even have to hire the stripling with the calculator over the skilled number expert of yesterday. But we must remain aware that we will be hiring technical skill without virtue, loyalty, or strength of character. For those qualities, we might do far better to hire the elderly accountant with the green eyeshade. Technology is very useful indeed, but it doesn't automatically produce greatness in people; sometimes it only conceals weakness. Not only that, but on occasion technological advance provides the illusion that we are moving forward when in reality we are sliding backward.

What does charity need, efficient technology or nice people?

If you want to produce inexpensive plastic boats you need nothing but machines and technical skills. If you want to produce works of wooden art, you need people who have been steeped in the wisdom of the past. Does helping the poor more closely resemble mass-producing plastic boats or is it more similar to shaping individually a unique masterpiece? To improve our ability to help other human beings, each unique in his need, do we need faster computers and electronic disbursement systems or do we need wiser and more experienced people who possess a deep understanding of human nature? To help a suffering person, do we need a committee of politicians, bureaucrats, and academics, or do we need caring humans whose very souls weep at the sight of pain?

Science can't decide who is poor

Those who desire to solve all human problems scientifically, by consulting the future rather than the past, try to identify those needing our help by applying objective parameters. After all, that long line of applicants does need to be sifted and distinctions made between those we consider worthy of our help and those who may be seeking the answer to gracious living and an easier alternative to work. How are we to distinguish? In our private charitable activities, we each use our own personal judgment about whom we wish to benefit with our largesse, but with a governmental system, we need a system that anyone can apply. Winston Churchill once said that the Royal Navy was a system designed by geniuses to be operated by idiots. The problem is that we have not yet found a large scale welfare system designed by geniuses. And those administering the system seldom fall into that category. So what are bureaucrats to do? They simply proclaim that all those earning below some named figure each year are henceforth designated "the poor". Alternatively, they capriciously label those taxpayers whose taxable income is in the lowest fifteen percent of the population to be "the poor".

Accordingly, the United States Census Bureau and the Commerce Department declare 30 million Americans to be living in poverty. Of these, government sources concede, 50 per cent own their own homes, 70 per cent own a car, while 30 per cent own two cars. Not to begrudge anyone anything, but 98 per cent of America's poor own a colour television while 50 per cent of them own two. 75 per cent of American poor own a video cassette recorder while 20 per cent own two video cassette recorders. 70per cent own a microwave and the same percentage own air-conditioning. While all this does not necessarily make for opulent living, it certainly describes a life style that about 80 per cent of the planet's inhabitants would change places with in a heartbeat.

This highlights precisely why science just isn't the right tool for solving poverty. It cannot even identify who the deserving poor are. It is like trying to use a Caterpillar bulldozer to shampoo your carpets; good tool, wrong job. Humans are different from all other creatures, which makes the task of identifying the unfortunate difficult. Furthermore, each human is different from every other human in important ways and this makes the task all but impossible.

I would go even further and say that trying to locate "the poor" or "the less fortunate" is impossible because they don't exist objectively as do, for instance, those people who have blue eyes. Eye colouring is an objectively measurable quantity, wealth and poverty are not. Here are three reasons why there is no such thing as "the poor".

Its classifications of poverty oversimplify and demonize the poor

Reason one is that human lives are more accurately depicted by videos than by snapshots. I may feel unhappy and unfulfilled today, however that in no way suggests that this is how I must also feel next week. I may be earning minimum wage this month, but if I keep my job and acquire skills, my employer won't want to risk losing me because replacing me and teaching someone else all over again is expensive. In order to retain my services he will undoubtedly pay me more next month. I may be a penniless student this year but next year, after qualifying as a lawyer, I shall have a job that quickly propels me into the top ten percent of the country's earners. There are people who are on the bottom rung of material success this year. However, having moved on up, they are not necessarily the same people who occupy that rung next year, thus there is not one group of chronically poor people. Most people's lives exhibit the escalator effect. Tomorrow's successful young lawyer should not make claims upon the generosity of today's fork-lift operator.

Human beings are not just smart animals, they are far more

Reason two is that humans are not animals. It is easy to identify poverty in a creature whose needs and desires are finite and predictable. Few obese animals are found in the wild because, for instance, every giraffe needs about forty pounds of vegetation each day. If a giraffe is given more greenery than his needs he will ignore the excess. If he obtains less than his needs, he could be called poor. However, with people it is quite different. One couple may choose to have many children, whom they prefer to educate in expensive private schools leaving them with very little discretionary income. In fact, they may live in somewhat run-down housing and seldom eat out in fancy restaurants. I would hesitate to term them poor and they themselves would indignantly reject the identification. At the same time, another couple with the same income may choose to live childless, in upscale circumstances. Are they rich enough to be asked to subsidize the large family? People make choices which come with consequences. One man may choose to work two jobs while going to night school to improve himself, while another values his leisure time and seldom works at all. Should the former be required to underwrite the lifestyle of the latter? Again it becomes impossible to identify the less fortunate objectively by numbers in any fashion that does not seem almost arbitrary.

Labelling people by materialistic parameters such as the colour of their skin or the size of their bank balance is cruel and wrong

Finally, we all tend to be as good as we believe we are. We attempt and we accomplish in proportion to our expectations of ourselves. Randomly labelling part of the population as poor therefore strikes me as cruelly condemning them to continuing their condition. No matter how straightened my personal financial circumstances may be, I do not want to be told by no less an authority than my government, that this condition which I view as temporary, is my actual identity. Calling me "poor" reduces me to a helpless victim of circumstance. As a very wealthy individual, I would also not wish to have my total human complexity and depth be dismissed with the label – "the rich". Again we see that it is very difficult if not impossible to produce a mathematical description that would identify the so-called poor. At very best, doing so is evil.

Jewish wisdom and poverty

Ancient Jewish wisdom provides an entirely different model for helping the less fortunate. First of all it accepts that everyone is unique and everyone will be different from everyone else. Some will be handsome and beautiful while others would possess ordinary appearances. Some would be healthier than others and yes, some would even be wealthier than others. This did not mean that the wealthy individual was nobler than the poor. Neither did it imply that the poor man was inherently nobler on account of his poverty.

It is of course easy to become discouraged by the presence of poverty and easy to write off the entire social and civic structure that seems to tolerate poverty in its midst. In fact, it is easy to fall into the trap of considering such a social and civic system intrinsically evil. Thus even today, as in years gone by, we sometimes tend to drape a mantle of virtue over those who rampage and riot against global trade. We assume that since poverty is allowed to exist in this growing global marketplace, we must find a better system. Ancient Jewish wisdom always derived its understanding of poverty from apparently contradictory Scriptures.

Surely there will be no destitute among you, God will bless you...but only if you hearken to the voice of the Lord your God.[237]

Alright, I think I understand. Follow the rules and there will be no poor people in your society. That sounds like a pretty good deal. Yet, no more than seven verses later we can read,

Destitute people will never cease to exist in your society, so I command you to always open your hand to your brother the poor.[238]

Well, which is it? Either by following the rules there will never be poor among us, or there will never be an end to poor people. Which is it?

The traditional answer, which always guided the most successful socio-economic systems, is that wealth and poverty are completely relative concepts. On other continents there are hundreds of millions of poor people who literally do not know where their next crust of bread is coming from and whether or not they will find shelter to lay their heads when the sun goes down. In the United States, by contrast, we can be amazed at the lifestyles of those upon whom we lavish our generous largesse. Obviously most poor people in Asia or Africa would leap at the chance to become part of America's poor. Am I suggesting that these thirty million Americans are not really poor? Of course not. Judaism teaches that poverty is relative. If one loses one's money and has to endure a dramatically reduced standard of living, one is poor according to Jewish definitions. What is more, such a person is a worthy charity recipient. If one owns one's own home with two colour televisions, two VCRs and a garage with two cars, but one lives among friends and associates all of whom live in far larger homes with many more amenities, then one is going to feel poor. That is the point of the two seemingly contradictory verses I mentioned earlier. Poverty is quite relative.

The sensitivity of traditional wisdom about poverty

That first Biblical verse insists that there will be no poor among you. That is right, if you live correctly, there is no reason for you ever to consider yourself poor. You are not to label yourself poor. You may have less than you used to once have. You may have less than those around you, but this is temporary. You are on your way up. You almost certainly have less than you could have tomorrow. Thinking of yourself as poor will handicap you in your quest. You can look over one shoulder and see many who possess far more than you. Do not allow this to make you see yourself as poor. Yes, there are many with more than you. So what? This does not make you poor. That is all there is to it. Do not be poor. Let nobody consider himself poor. That is an order!

The second verse is telling us that now that you are not poor, look over your other shoulder and see all those unfortunate souls with less than you. Now open your hands to them and share. This credo is so strongly established that even people who depend upon charity for their livelihood are obliged to give charity to those who have even less.

The contradiction is resolved. Let nobody consider himself to be poor. Forming that opinion of yourself erects an insurmountable obstacle to becoming rich. If nobody allows a self image of being poor, then the first verse is correct, there will be no poor among you. However, there will always be some people with less than you. They must not consider themselves poor, but you are obliged to give something to those with less than you.[239]

This is one of the best reasons for why helping the less fortunate must be the obligation of individuals and not made an obligation of government. No government, no foundation and no board of directors, no matter how well-meaning, can identify the poor let alone actually help them. What is more, when governments attempt this impossible task, not only do they invariably fail, but they discourage individuals from helping the less fortunate. Why should I help the Smiths down the block when so much of my income is already taxed to help them? Let the Smiths go down to the Welfare Office like everyone else. The futile government programme only serves to exempt from the challenge the very people who could actually do something about it.

Experts often lack this sensitivity

Many parents become intimidated by experts. For instance there was a period when experts decreed not only the ideal number of years that parents should wait for spacing children but even how many children couples should plan on having. A glance at the literature shows that only a few years later the experts were still dispensing this advice but their recommendations had entirely changed. On this topic, parents simply do not need advice from the latest issue of some magazine. Instead they might consider advice from their parents or grandparents.

Universities these days have changed their mission from producing great graduates steeped in the wisdom of human experience to becoming technical institutes. Now there is nothing wrong with a technical institute. One of the very right things about a technical institute is that it produces technically skilled people not experts with doctoral degrees. Nobody dreams of allowing his plumber or mechanic to tell him how to run his marriage or whether or not to take his children to church. Unfortunately many feel insecure in making these decisions without having their views confirmed by someone with a graduate degree in psychology.

When we hand off responsibility for our entire relationship with money and those who have less than we do to experts in government and academia we do ourselves a disservice. Not only do we deprive our lives of the richness that flows from personally determining these matters and acting on our convictions, we end up empowering the powerless.

Our relationship with money and with other people who have both more and less than we do is incredibly complex. When I choose to bestow my charity upon a particular individual or family, I am not merely dispatching an anonymous cheque. Whether through my institute of religious affiliation or whether through my civic service club, I do far more than that. I am also creating a relationship with other human beings. I am able to judge worthiness, I am able to judge urgency, and I am able to determine when my help is no longer needed. None of this can be done by a machine or by an impersonal agency of the kind that governments tend to create. In making these judgments and determinations, I depend upon my experience and upon my handed-down wisdom rather than upon my computer. I depend upon my values and the things I believe in rather than in objective facts and impersonal statistics.

In a medical emergency I need an expert. I also value experts who can analyse bond yields, experts who can network computers, and experts who can repair the engines of BMW motor cars. I do not need an expert to tell me how to relate to my ageing parents, neither do I need an expert to tell me how to relate to those less fortunate than me.

Some things don't change and wisdom is one

The more that things change, the more we must depend on those things that never change. My great-grandfather worked about ten hours a day. So do I. Admittedly his ten hours spent in close proximity to a blast furnace was considerably less pleasant and more arduous than mine in front of a computer keyboard and a telephone. But ten hours of work in order to earn a living is pretty much ten hours of work. It is certainly a large slice of each day during which I am not at liberty to do what I would really prefer doing. That is as true for me as it was for great-grandpa.

At the end of his workday, he sank into the pile of straw he considered a bed with no less enthusiasm than that with which I tumble onto my thermostatically-heated water bed. He took as much pleasure in his wife as I do and regarded his children to be as important as his next breath just as I do. His young children spent their leisure hours kicking a ball down the street while mine play video games, but he educated them morally as well as technically just as I try to do. He was away from home on business about as much as I am. He travelled smaller distances than I do and he travelled by wagon while I travel by jet. However, like me, he found travel far less comfortable than being home and he kept on doing it for precisely the same reason I do. The real joys in his life came from exactly the same sources as do mine and his deep disappointments shared much with mine. My life is a lot safer and a lot more comfortable than his was; he could not imagine the things I take for granted. However, it is easy to see that our lives are far more similar than they are different provided we don't allow technological pyrotechnics to obscure the fundamental similarities.

Many other things remain more similar than different. For instance, our human yearning to travel and thereby overcome the frustrating limitations of space and time, has always been part of our nature. Whether we fulfilled those yearnings in each epoch by means of a camel, a canoe, a Cadillac or a Concorde really makes little difference. Similarly we ought to recognize the universal aspects of wealth and poverty. In every epoch there have been those with more than others and those with less. Identicalness is not part of the human condition. Even our faces and fingerprints announce our utter, special, uniqueness. Some are endowed with great intelligence while others are far more average. Just as some will win the ovarian lottery and grow up to be extraordinarily healthy and beautiful while others will be just average, some will acquire assets in greater number while others just get by. The approaches used by our ancestors to deal with issues of wealth and poverty might well turn out to be more effective than those advanced today. The way that our fathers attempted to solve the problems that surround helping the less fortunate might be more effective than those we use today. They could hardly be any worse.

CHAPTER 9

Punishing criminals

Graeme Newman

On crime and its punishment

And he that smiteth any man mortally shall surely be put to death.
And he that smiteth a beast mortally shall make it good, life for life.
And if a man cause a blemish in his neighbour; as he hath done, so
shall it be done to him: breach for breach, eye for eye, tooth for tooth; as
he hath caused a blemish in a man, so shall it be rendered unto him.[240]

The role of punishment in criminal justice today has become impossibly obscured. The simplicity of the Old Testament offers an attractive solution. Today's criminal justice system is dominated in America and elsewhere by complex "sentencing guidelines", a set of options for punishments of all combinations of crimes and aggravating or mitigating factors that the judge must follow. And in England we believe it is dominated by the accumulated wisdom of common law. But there is no such accumulated wisdom, though many accumulated cases. The "wisdom" we have today is largely that of the technical solution of prison, with the artificial computation of days, months or years to match any particular crime. It is a technical or artificial solution to the problem of matching a punishment to its crime because it provides only an illusory solution to this intractable problem. What is the qualitative difference between two years prison and three years prison? And how does one find the point of contact between a set amount of prison and a particular crime? For example, if a robbery is worth one year in prison, what are two robberies worth? Worse, if a robbery is worth one year in prison, what is a rape worth, or a burglary worth? There is no known way of determining the comparative seriousness of these crimes (not to mention the many aggravating and mitigating circumstances that always accompany them). The incredible range of sentences typically given for crimes in different countries and jurisdictions within countries attests to this fact. For example, in the United States it is possible to receive two years probation for a homicide in New York City, but life in prison for cheque forgery in Texas.

Older solutions making punishments fit crimes

If we followed to the letter the Old Testament advocacy of an eye for an eye, we would be charged with seeking vengeance or bloody revenge; the claim being that vengeance is "uncivilized". Here is the obfuscation. Our forefathers really did try to match the punishment to the crime in a literal sense. Rapists were hanged on the spot where they committed the crime. Hester Prynne wore an "A" on her breast to depict her adultery. Thieves and other criminals had the first letter of their crime branded on parts of their body. Others had the particular part of their body identified as the seat of the crime either mutilated or removed (the tongue of a blasphemer, the hand of a thief). Our refined sensibilities no longer allow us to do such things, even though there could be good reason to do so in some cases, such as castration of sexual predators. But if the latter is acceptable (and in some jurisdictions and countries it is) why isn't mutilation of other parts of the body acceptable?

Prison does not match punishment to crime

How, then, to match a punishment to its crime? The examples of old time punishments offer one way to solve this puzzle: to link the details of the punishment as closely as possible to the details of the crime. The punishment should reflect elements of the crime itself: the place of the crime, the part of the body responsible for committing the crime. It is surely obvious that to place all offenders in prison for a huge variety of crimes stands no chance of matching the punishment to the crime, since all prisoners receive the same type of punishment irrespective of the crime they committed. There is only the pretence of matching the punishment to the crime by adjusting the amount of time spent in prison. But time is incredibly abstract, and has no concrete meaning as a punishment, and certainly no relationship to most crimes that are committed. Can't we apply the old time idea of matching the punishment to the crime in a modern way? It requires a great deal of creativity, and the discipline to emphasize the quality of the punishment rather than its quantity. Consider some examples of actual sentences delivered by some creative judges:

CRIME: A man rams his truck into a car driven by an interracial couple.
SENTENCE: Watch the movie "Mississippi Burning".

CRIME: Drunken driving.
SENTENCE: Clean elephant cages at the local zoo.

CRIME: Shoplifter who was also a singer.
SENTENCE: Must do four concerts for senior citizens.

CRIME: Snow-plough operator convicted of several driving offences.
SENTENCE: Plough parking lot of the American Cancer Society.

CRIME: Drunk driver crashes truck, kills ten of his friends.
SENTENCE: Three years volunteer work in local hospital emergency unit.

CRIME: Trafficker in pornography.
SENTENCE: Ordered to donate 3,000 "clean" books to local library.

CRIME: White man harasses interracial couple.
SENTENCE: 50 weekends working in a black church.

CRIME: Neurosurgeon refuses court order to clean up apartment properties he owns.
SENTENCE: Ordered to spend 30 days in one of his own unclean apartments.

CRIME: Two teenagers set fire to a car.
SENTENCE: Ordered to write 1,000 times, "I will not destroy property of another person, because it is wrong".

CRIME: Trafficking in cocaine.

SENTENCE: Ordered to watch autopsies of drug over-dose victims.

The sentences related above are generally for minor offences, or when applied to serious offences, give the impression that they are not severe enough. Yet when we see punishments that fully reflect the crime, that truly demonstrate that the punishment matched the crime (that is, the criminal "got what he deserved"), we experience an undeniable feeling of satisfaction. It reflects an appreciation that justice has been done. That something good or even "beautiful" (one is reminded of the term "poetic justice") has occurred is surely undeniable. The sentences related above are brave attempts to match the punishment to the crime according to the old idea of deserts. Only in one or two of them do we experience any reaction that approaches the satisfaction that justice has been accomplished. This lack of appreciation is not so much because of the failure of the judge to create a sentence that reflects the crime, but rather because we ourselves have lost our sense of how to match a punishment to its crime.

On time: not a good way of calibrating punishment

A starving fox found some bread and cheese inside a hollow oak tree. He squeezed his way in through a small space and gorged himself. However, his stomach had swollen so much with the food that he could not get out again. So he wailed and moaned. A shepherd who had left the bread and cheese came by to retrieve it. He listened to the fox's lament, and said: "Ah well! Stay where you are until you become the size that you were when you climbed in, and then you will be able to get out easily enough."[241]

Time heals all, so the saying goes. But not completely. In the modern age – that is for about the last two hundred years – time has become the major tool for punishing crime. It is the essential ingredient of prison and of its less serious offspring probation, community service, and parole. Yet we know that, unlike the fox, whose guiding principle is more likely "once bitten twice shy", criminals do not learn from their mistakes. Depending on the country or culture, roughly over 70 per cent of all offenders sent to prison commit another offence within several years after release. Why is this? Aesop told another fable that provides the explanation:

One winter a kind farmer found a snake stiff with cold. He placed it under his shirt and warmed it against his chest. The snake revived, and on doing so, struck out and killed its benefactor. When he realized he was dying, the man said: "I well deserve it for taking pity on a wicked wretch."[242]

As Aesop's commentators say, in adding the moral to this story:

The perversity of nature does not change under the influence of kindness.

We might add, nor does it change under the influence of punishment.

On eliminating punishment

Let us eliminate the concept of sin from the world – and let us soon dispatch the concept of punishment after it![243]

That man be delivered from revenge, that to me is the bridge to the highest hope...[244]

Ye have heard that it was said, An eye for an eye, and a tooth for a tooth: but I say unto you, Resist not him that is evil: but whosoever smiteth thee on thy right cheek, turn to him the other also. And if any man would...take away thy coat, let him have thy cloak also.[245]

These quotations from Nietzsche and Jesus appear to express the same values: punishment, especially in return for an evil, is also evil. Consistent with his philosophy, Nietzsche's proclamation goes far beyond that of Jesus. For he argues that the way to eradicate punishment is to eradicate sin. How is this possible? The assumption is that punishment is the product of sin, so abolishing sin would abolish punishment. But how does one abolish sin? Nietzsche tried to do it by proclamation. His many philosophical tracts argued for the abolition of established morality, to go beyond good and evil, to deny especially the values of the Judeao-Christian philosophy. Can one abolish evil simply by saying that it no longer exists? Yet even if all people are convinced by the argument, does it follow that people's behaviour will be such that it does not invite a punitive response? The extensive research of the neo-Darwinians shows clearly that reciprocal behaviour among many animal species from single celled organisms to chimps and humans does not follow Nietzsche's pronouncement, and is not likely to given the several hundred million years it has taken for such behaviour patterns to evolve. The social relationships among individuals of many species revolve around the principle of reciprocity: that is, "tit-for-tat". If you hit me, I hit you back. If you do me a good turn, I do one for you. The golden rule has a deep biological source:

Do unto others as you would have done unto you.

Jesus takes the idea of reciprocity one step further by advocating an asymmetrical reciprocity. One returns, not a wrong for a wrong, but a good for a wrong (if my coat is stolen I offer up as well my cloak). Christians throughout the ages have struggled to live up to this seemingly impossible exhortation.

Yet evolutionists have discovered that individuals in many species also practise what they call reciprocal altruism. Individuals, often parents or relatives, will risk their own lives when attacked in order to save those of others dear to them. Is this what Jesus was advocating when he urged individuals to turn the other cheek when wronged? Surely to do so in the dangerous and predatory modern world would be equivalent to bearing one's throat to the attacker? In fact, evolutionists have found through computer simulations of artificial life that a complex combination of both aspects of reciprocity contribute to the most evolutionarily stable societies. That is, societies need both the punitive tit-for-tat, and the occasional asymmetrical response of turning the other cheek. Evolutionists have found from their computer simulations that, if everyone turns the other cheek, society is overrun by predators and quickly self-destructs. The Bible taken overall, reflects this truth. The Old Testament urges an eye for an eye (symmetrical reciprocity) and the New Testament urges turn the other cheek (asymmetrical reciprocity).

On criminal excuses

Kill her, take her money, dedicate it to serving mankind, to the general welfare...For one life thousands of lives saved from ruin or collapse…What does the life of this sickly, stupid, bad-tempered old woman mean anyway in the balance of existence? No more than the life of a louse or a cockroach. Not that much – because the old woman actually does harm. She eats up other people's lives.[246]

The human capacity for deception, especially self-deception, knows no bounds. Dostoyevsky's torn character, Raskolnikov – smart young man, intelligent, very caring for his family especially for his sister – can't resist the idea of committing a murder simply because he wants to show the world and himself that he has the "moral" strength to do it. Just about every generation complains of the moral decay of the younger generation. Raskolnikov was very much devoted to the many moral requirements of his age, especially those of honour and duty to his family. But he was also well educated and steeped in the philosophical arguments of his day. And any good education worth its salt, whether religious or secular, will challenge a student to question the logical and factual basis of current and past truths. It is an important part of intellectual growing up. Almost all students (indeed all people) mature through the questioning stage and settle down with a sense of respect for human life and a sense of the continuity of values embedded in human nature. The values that support and protect the integrity of human life are not hidden or even complicated. Raskolnikov's obsessive ruminations made them complicated, though, and he found that he had to go through many self-deceptions (the truths of which were often revealed to him in dreams and nightmares) in order to convince himself that he could carry out a murder that he basically knew was wrong and criminal.

The modern expression for Raskolnikov's thinking is called denial of the victim. And the mechanism for achieving this denial is called neutralization. Raskolnikov convinced himself that his victim – a wicked pawnbroker – deserved to die because she lived like a parasite on the backs of her suffering clients. He even redefined her as less than human – an insect – which further neutralized the moral and legal proscription against her murder. This was, he concluded, a justifiable homicide. There are many examples of this thinking among those who plan to commit crimes, or who try to justify them after the fact:

SHOPLIFTING: "The candy was placed right at checkout where I couldn't help but take it. The shopkeeper is just asking for it to be taken."

COMPUTER CRIME: "I just did it for fun and the challenge. I didn't hurt anyone." The cost of computer crime and hacking is estimated to be $1.6 trillion a year.

GRAFFITI: "People don't realize that what we do is art just as good as you see in fancy galleries. They don't like it because we are poor."

COPYRIGHT VIOLATION, COUNTERFEITING: "The corporations rip people off all the time. This is a way of getting back."

CRIMES AGAINST BUSINESS: "Businesses have loads of money. They won't even notice the loss."

HOMICIDE: "He asked for it. I had to defend my honour."

ROBBERY AND BURGLARY: "Capitalism exploits the poor. I'm just evening up the score."

DRUNK DRIVING: "I can hold my booze. I never had an accident."

TAX EVASION: "Everybody does it."

NEUTRALIZATION AFTER THE CRIME:
"I don't remember anything."
"I was suffering depression."
"My husband abused me for so long I just couldn't stand it any more, so I killed him."
"My father abused me as a child."
"My friends, family members, made me do it."
"I didn't know the gun was loaded."
"I had a few too many drinks."

Crime and everyday life

Town Rat invited his friend Country Rat to his house for a holiday, promising him the best of times, wonderful food, lush living. Country Rat arrived, and was treated to a sumptuous feast and a grand party. But the party was broken up by a nasty sound of Cat which made

148

Town Rat, with Country Rat right on his heels, scurry to his hole.
When the Cat had gone, Town Rat said, "Come on, let's go out and
party."

"Count me out", the rustic said.
"Be my guest tomorrow where,
Though I do not say I'm fed
On your sort of royal fare,

"No intruder interrupts,
And I eat my food at leisure.
Good night; not for me the pleasure
That a breath of fear corrupts."[247]

Throughout history ordinary people have made many adjustments in their lives to cope with crime. The great castles in the countryside protected the inhabitants against attacks from without, and could be a place of refuge for farmers in times of danger. The walled cities of the middle ages and before were a defence against predators. But they also enclosed the people inside the walls and forced a view of danger as coming from outside rather than within. As urban life began, the problems of crime arose as a direct result of lifestyles that emerged. Houses were designed with limited entry from the street, and activity centred on a courtyard inside. Apartment buildings rose and had, as a matter of course, persons whose job it was to monitor entry and exit of the building. Such arrangements exist in large cities all over the world. And even in the countryside, there are now "gated communities" where suburban life exists behind walls and security guards.

The twenty-first century brings with it the promise of further changes to our lifestyles made in direct response to the activities of criminals. There are car alarms, car radios with electronic keys that render them useless if stolen, electronic tagging of products so their ownership can be easily identified, direction finders and locators so that not only criminals with ankle bracelets can be found, but also so that car rentals can be tracked, or even privately owned cars can be located if stolen. Closed circuit television has been widely introduced in many public places in the United Kingdom and elsewhere. People have become used to their everyday lives being more and more monitored. Electronic recognition of cars moving through toll payment booths so they do not have to stop for payment is widespread. Now, even our travel on public highways is monitored and recorded. Automatic red light and speed cameras are common place in many parts of England, Australia, the USA and Europe.

Do you lock your house when you leave for work each day? Do you lock your car? Do you keep your hand on your wallet or handbag when shopping? Do you look furtively behind you to see who is there when walking down a street, especially a quiet street? Do you write your name inside each book you buy? Write your name on your luggage, put name tags on your kids' things that they take to school? All of these everyday acts are caused by the threat of crime. We do them mostly without thinking.

On rehabilitation

Is a man who chooses the bad in some way better than a man who has the good imposed upon him?[248]

It has been said that a person who is saved, after having fallen from the moral path, is somehow more saintly than one who has never fallen. For it is assumed that one who falls by the wayside did so of his own doing. He or she made a choice, gave in to temptation, or even felt forced into a deviant lifestyle because of economic or cultural conditions of life. Prostitutes are the favourite characters of novelists (Dostoyevsky's Sofya who hears Raskolnikov's confession) to portray this view of morality. Only after having experienced a wayward life, after having fallen so low, could a person truly understand the common sins and defects of ordinary humans who have not fallen so far. Such "born again" individuals see more clearly human values and the inevitable suffering embedded in the temptations of everyday life. They have a greater capacity, it seems, for forgiveness.

But modern rehabilitation programmes rarely focus on having the criminal comprehend how low he has fallen, and forcing him to acknowledge the depravity of his acts. Rather, they are directed at the superficialities of promises from the offender that he will not repeat his offence, rewards given for good behaviour in prison (eg, early parole), mutual reinforcement of each others' behaviour through "group therapy", recognition of "prisoners' rights" and even the bargaining between the offender and the prosecutor over the crime they will both accept as the one the offender committed which may or may not bear any resemblance to the crime actually committed. This process, endemic to criminal justice systems in many parts of the modern world, ignores the prime responsibility of the criminal for his deeds, and debases the moral underpinning of the crime which is – or ought to be – the concern for the inherent evil of the criminal act and the damage done to innocent victims.

Thus, in *A Clockwork Orange* the protagonist Alex, a young thug who perpetrates unspeakable violence against innocent victims, is whisked away from a prison where he was placed for the rest of his life, and offered early release once he undergoes an experimental program of cure. The cure would be conditioning against violence, using drugs that make him painfully nauseated whenever he had violent thoughts. How does this treatment compare to a lifetime in prison for a brutal rape and murder? His suffering amounted to about two weeks of painful conditioning, but after that he could return to a "normal life". Does this treatment match the crime? Is it a punishment worthy of the crime? Can he be considered "cured" even though, if he could, he would still choose violence, but is simply prevented from doing so by a physical reaction that he cannot control? The criminal under such circumstances has not been rehabilitated at all – certainly not saved from the depths of criminality. For his responsibility for the crime has been ignored. Only the suppression of his violent behaviour is valued. If he had a choice, he would still choose murder. But he can't, because he has had the "good imposed upon him".

On becoming a victim of crime

Two mules, good friends, ambled down the road, one carrying oats, the other silver. The mule with silver strutted with pride and vanity. Suddenly, robbers appeared on the road and immediately made for the silver, mercilessly beating the mule. "Why have they attacked me so? What did I do to deserve this?" Spoke the unhappy victim. His friend carrying the oats replied:
"My friend,
Big jobs don't always prove to be so fine.
Were you but doing a miller's work like mine,

Your malady might sooner mend."[249]

The primary responsibility for a crime of course lies with the perpetrator. However, a criminal selects as his target from among many possible victims depending on the crime and the circumstances. While we would not want to suggest that those who become victims of crime "asked for it", nevertheless there is good reason to ask the question, do those who become victims of crime bear any responsibility for becoming so? This question can be answered positively in regard to a number of different kinds of crimes. Here are some examples:

SHOPLIFTING: A shoplifter should of course be apprehended and punished for his offence. But do not shopkeepers exploit the weaknesses of their customers by displaying attractive goods under the noses of customers, often without surveillance, and in large quantities?

SERIAL MURDER: A serial killer, we well know, hunts for his victims just like a tiger hunting for prey. He will survey the field and choose the prey that is easiest to catch – alone, away from its group, weaker than the rest, easier to subdue. This is why children are often such victims, as are women, and those who hitch rides on lonely roads.

CAR THEFT: Certain models of cars are much more likely to be stolen than others. The most stolen cars in America in 2000, in order from most to least were:

1. Toyota Camry
2. Honda Accord
3. Oldsmobile Cutlass
4. Honda Civic
5. Jeep Cherokee/Grand Cherokee
6. Chevrolet Full Size C/K pick-up
7. Toyota Corolla
8. Chevrolet Caprice
9. Ford Taurus
10. Ford F150 pick-up

Is it a characteristic of the thief or a characteristic of the car that invites this discriminating victimization? We know that some cars are much easier to steal than others. We also know that many owners do not lock their vehicles.

BURGLARY: The most commonly stolen items in burglaries are expensive electronic items such as VCRs, TVs and jewellery. Naturally, those houses that are most likely to stand out as containing such items – just as the mule flaunted his load of silver – are more likely to be victimized.

RAPE: She didn't "ask for it". But if she displays her wares, as did the mule, she runs the risk of being selected by a predator.

BANK ROBBERY: One bank has electronically controlled door entry and strengthened glass partitions between teller and customer. Another bank has none. Which bank is most likely to be robbed?

PRODUCT VICTIMIZATION: Many products, simply because they are the kinds of products they are, just ask to be stolen. These are products that are small, fashionable, easily concealed on the person, and easily disposed of. The most popular target of such theft today is a mobile phone, especially because it brings with it access to a whole range of services. Other products are selectively victimized not by theft but by vandalism, misuse and abuse. The Mercedes badge so prominent on the front of the prestigious Mercedes Benz was for many years the target of theft and vandalism. Certain prescription drugs can be misused for criminal purposes, simply because they are packaged in the way they are. For example, the drug OxyContin, a time-release pain relieving drug, if bitten open can give the immediate equivalent of six or more regular doses. Many over the counter medicines are now tamper-proofed to prevent product tampering as happened in the Tylenol case in the USA in 1982. The open display and insecure packaging of these items made them vulnerable to crime.

On policing crime

A child stole a writing tablet from one of his classmates and took it home to his mother. She thanked him for the gift. He continued to steal many other items, and brought them home to his mother. When he came of age, he stole many important and expensive items which he also gave to his mother. But he was eventually caught in the act and led off to the executioner. His mother went to him, wailing and crying. Her son called to her to come close, he would like to whisper something in her ear. She did so. And her son bit off her ear. She reproached him bitterly, and he replied: "If you had thrashed me the first time I brought home the stolen writing tablet I would not now be facing death."[250]

The lesson of this fable can be applied to many different aspects of crime and punishment. However, the most recent application is to policing, expressed in the idea of "zero tolerance". A seminal study a decade ago found that in neighbourhoods that were run down – the houses were not looked after, gardens were unkempt, the streets poorly maintained – crime of every kind was more abundant. This in itself was no great discovery. After all, criminologists (and ordinary people as well) have known for a long time that run down neighbourhoods are places where crime flourishes. But the interesting aspect of this study was that a concerted effort was made to clean up streets and neighbourhoods – to mend broken windows and create a climate of decency. The mere cleaning up of these "superficial" aspects of neighbourhoods contributed significantly to the reduction of all kinds of crime, not just vandalism, which was the most common crime thought to be encouraged by poorly maintained houses and buildings. Could the idea be applied to other settings? Perhaps policing seemingly smaller quality of life aspects of people's behaviour – smaller offences such as jay-walking, jumping the turn-style in the subway – crimes of greater severity might decline? In fact, when this approach was applied in New York City, this effect was found. Policing all around the world has come to realize that nipping trouble in the bud can have far reaching effects in preventing the occurrence of serious crime. The trouble is, some citizens have complained that this level of policing reaches too far into the everyday lives of good citizens whose occasional minor deviations from the law are subject to close scrutiny. It seems that they are paying a heavier price for the prevention of crime than are the real criminals.

Growing old

Robert Grant

Plato and growing old

Though not professionally qualified in this subject, I can at least claim some personal experience of it. Until well into middle age I enjoyed almost obscenely robust health. But once (as in my case) aches and pains come constantly and naggingly to accompany most of one's bodily movements, one's outlook begins to change. The pains of age, curiously, make one far more conscious of one's embodied condition, which is to say of one's transitoriness, than the pleasures of youth, even though those are customarily thought of – for example, by W B Yeats in "Sailing to Byzantium", to which I shall come – as pre-eminently "physical".

Few in the past survived into old age, and many who did died of diseases to which they could equally well have succumbed when young. Before modern medicine the longest lives of which we had any firm record, together with systematic reflection upon them, were those of classical antiquity. Like almost all classical literature, that on growing old is implicitly aristocratic, though it is also notable for recognizing that not everyone, especially the humbler classes, enjoys the writer's own good fortune, and of course that in the end death is the great leveller. The Greek and Roman élites enjoyed considerable longevity, owing to what even in modern terms was a very high standard of living. So for them to reflect on growing old made sense, whereas poorer people, even if they were literate and had access to writing materials, would probably have seen little point in anticipating what, for them, was an unlikely contingency.

There are many depictions in classical poetry and drama, some but not all of them flattering, of old age: Nestor, Odysseus's father Laertes,

Oedipus at Colonus, Alcestis' revoltingly mean-spirited old father-in-law Pheres; and countless others, many, as in Plautus, comic. The Roman poet Horace usually speaks of old age as either miserable (in a man) or disgusting (in a once desirable woman), and therefore as being, like death, something best put out of mind. Perhaps the most celebrated (and affirmative) philosophical treatments are Plato's, in the opening pages of the *Republic*, and Cicero's, in his short treatise *De Senectute* (On Old Age).

Plato's speaker Socrates recounts how he has just visited the rich, aged Cephalus at the Piraeus (my abridgement, ellipses unmarked):

He welcomed me eagerly, and then said: You don't come to see me, Socrates, as often as you ought: For if I were able to go and see you I would not ask you to come to me. But at my age I can hardly get to the city, and therefore you should come oftener to the Piraeus. For I find that as the pleasures and delights of the body fade, the love of discourse grows upon me.

I replied: There is nothing I like better, Cephalus, than conversing with aged men like yourself. And I should like to ask you: Is life harder towards the end, or what report do you give of it?

I will tell you, Socrates, he said. Old men flock together; and at our meetings the tale of my acquaintance commonly is: I cannot eat, I cannot drink; the pleasures of youth and love are fled, and now life is no longer life. Some lament over the slights put upon them by their relations, and will tell you plaintively of how many evils old age is the cause. But I do not believe, Socrates, that the blame is where they say; for if old age were the cause, I and every other old man would have felt the same. This, however, is not my own experience, nor that of others. I remember the aged poet Sophocles, when in answer to the question, How does love suit with age, Sophocles – are you still the man you were? Peace, he replied; most gladly have I escaped that, and I feel as if I had escaped from a mad and furious master. That saying has often come into my mind since. For certainly old age has a great sense of calm and freedom; when the passions relax their hold, then, as Sophocles says, you have escaped from the control not of one master only, but of many. And of these regrets, as well as of the complaint about relations, Socrates, the cause is to be sought, not in men's ages, but in their characters and

*tempers; for he who is of a calm and happy nature will hardly feel the
pressure of age, but an opposite disposition will find youth and age
equally a burden.*

*I was delighted at his words, and went on to say: Yes, Cephalus, but I
suspect that people in general think that old age sits lightly upon you,
not because of your happy disposition, but because wealth is a great
comforter.*

*That is true, he replied, and there is something in what they say; not,
however, so much as they imagine. Themistocles answered the Seriphian
who was abusing him and saying that he was famous, not for his own
merits but because he was an Athenian: "If you had been an Athenian
and I a Seriphian, neither of us would have been famous." And to those
who are not rich and are impatient of old age, the same reply may be
made; for neither can a good poor man lightly bear age, nor can a bad
rich man ever be at peace with himself.*

Socrates asks whether Cephalus inherited his wealth or made it, and,
hearing that it was mostly made, continues:

*That was why I asked, I said, because I saw that you were not fond of
money, which is a characteristic rather of those who have inherited
their fortunes than of those who have acquired them; for the latter have
a second or extraordinary love of money, resembling the affection of
authors for their own poems, or of parents for their children. And hence
they are very bad company, for they talk about nothing but wealth.*

Socrates then asks Cephalus: What do you consider to be the greatest
blessing which you have reaped from wealth?

*Not one, he said, of which I could easily convince others. For, Socrates,
when a man thinks himself near death he has fears which have never
entered his mind before. The tales of a life below and the punishment
there of deeds done here were a laughing matter to him once, but now
he is haunted with the thought that they may be true. But he who is
conscious of no sin has in age a sweet hope which, as Pindar charmingly
says, is a kind nurse to him. And this is the great blessing of riches to a
good man, that he has had no occasion to deceive another; and when*

he departs to the other world he is not in any apprehension about offerings due to the gods or debts to men. Therefore I say that this is to a man of sense the greatest of the many advantages which wealth has to give.[251]

It is remarkable that Cephalus, a man now too old to travel to Athens, says so little about the purely physical comforts and conveniences which the aged need more than the young, and which money can buy. But as we shall see, there are those, notably Wordsworth, who can find something dignified and comforting even in extreme destitution (others', it should be said).

Cicero

While adding his own observations, Cicero recycles some of Plato's, including the stories about Sophocles and Themistocles, without crediting Plato with them, but let that pass. Like Plato he stresses character as the decisive factor in whether age is tolerable or even advantageous. His imagined speakers are Scipio the Younger – here indeed young, but later to conquer Hannibal – and Cato the Elder, now eighty-four (abridgement and ellipses as previously):

S: I have noticed that old age never seemed a burden to you, while to most old men it is heavier than Etna.

C: Men, my dear Scipio, who have no resources in themselves for securing a good and happy life find every age burdensome. But those who look for all happiness from within can never think anything bad which Nature makes inevitable. In that category before anything else comes old age, to which all wish to attain, and at which all grumble when attained. Such is Folly's inconsistency!

Cato goes on to observe that:

the arms best adapted to old age are culture and the active exercise of the virtues, not only because they never fail us even in our last days, but also because the consciousness of a well-spent life and the recollection of many virtuous actions are exceedingly delightful.[252]

Cephalus was glad merely to be delivered from fear; but it is doubtless Cicero's thoroughgoing Stoicism (a post-Platonic philosophy) which has made him vicariously so self-complacent, like (some would say) Aristotle's "great-souled man". This impressive personage enjoys a firm, quasi-objective consciousness of his own indubitable worth, such as, for better or worse, no thinker of the Christian or even post-Christian era, except perhaps Nietzsche (rootedly sceptical though he was in other respects), could easily entertain. "There are four reasons", Cato continues, "for old age being thought unhappy":

> *first, that it withdraws us from active employments; second, that it enfeebles the body; third, that it deprives us of nearly all physical pleasures; fourth, that it is the next step to death.*

Needless to say, all are quasi-effortlessly shown to be either groundless or misconceived: the employments that matter are intellectual ones, such as public affairs; for them physical strength is unnecessary; physical pleasures are either overrated or a form of slavery (here Cato fields the Sophocles story); and the fear of death is irrational. (Yes, Philip Larkin would say, and that is just why it is so terrible. Of him, more anon.)

All these thoughts are or have become commonplaces, which is not to say that they are false. But Cato says other things of a practical nature, so that some of the discourse resembles a contemporary advice column for the elderly. He stresses the importance for old people of a healthy regimen, both physically, through moderate exercise and diet, and intellectually: "the intellect becomes nimbler by exercising itself". As we might recommend gardening, so he, lyrically, hymns the pleasures of farming and viticulture: "these are not hindered by old age, and seem to me to approach nearest to the ideal wise man's life". Old men should also have clubs, for dining and drinking of course (in moderation, naturally), but primarily for the pleasure of conviviality, which hospitality also encourages: "every day we have a full dinner-party of neighbours, which we prolong as far into the night as we can with varied conversation". Not bad at eighty-four, eh?

A final point of interest in Cicero is the idea, common to all traditional societies, European or otherwise, that the old, if they take care to deserve it, have a special place in society reserved for them by nature. The consul and censor Appius Claudius, though old and blind,

> *maintained not merely an influence but an absolute command over his family: his slaves feared him, his sons were in awe of him, all loved him. In that family, indeed, ancestral custom and discipline were in full vigour. The fact is that old age is respectable just as long as it asserts itself, maintains its proper rights, and is not enslaved to anyone. For as I admire a young man who has something of the old man in him, so do I an old one who has something of a young man. The man who aims at this may possibly become old in body – in mind he never will.*

Cato then describes his intellectual interests in old age – history, antiquarianism, literary composition, collecting and publishing his speeches, learning Greek – and says:

> *For a man who is always living in the midst of these studies and labours does not perceive when old age creeps upon him. Thus, by slow and imperceptible degrees life draws to its end. There is no sudden breakage; it just slowly goes out.*

If only it were always so.

Shakespeare

Shakespeare has a number of portraits of the old, few of them idealized, and testifying overall to a broader grasp than either Plato or Cicero: Falstaff, Shylock, Polonius, Lear, Duncan, Prospero. The most interesting for present purposes are King Lear and Prospero. Lear is vain, silly, wilful and impulsive, and determined to eat his cake and have it, that is, in dividing and giving away his kingdom, at once to renounce his responsibility yet retain his authority. In consequence he soon finds himself powerless and humiliated, and his country (ancient Britain) at war. He is what a foolish Prospero might have been. To have brought him finally to self-knowledge, and us to sympathizing with him, is an artistic triumph. In Prospero, however, we see wisdom, magnanimity, self-mastery, and a grateful acceptance of the providential order. He needs them all, knowing himself to have (like Lear) an irritable, peremptory, authoritarian streak. But they also enable and qualify him to exercise the benign authority (and power) that others' moral education requires. Once he has brought those others to repentance, or maturity, or autonomy – what he calls "their proper selves" – so that his power over them is no longer needed, he can set them and himself free, and this he does, when he finally destroys his magician's staff and books and returns to Milan and normality, where "every third thought shall be my grave".

The contrasting views of old age as either fearsome and horrible, or venerable and rewarding, are as old as humanity, so that one would conclude even without first-hand evidence that, first, both can be true, because old age itself varies from person to person; and secondly, that one's view greatly depends on the disposition one brings to the task. Thirdly, it will naturally be coloured by one's own experience or lack of it. In general, one is faced with a paradox. Wisdom about old age may not always be the same as the truth about it. The wisest course of all, resignation, may sometimes be impossible. Or it may be enforced, or indistinguishable from misery, like that of the dying octogenarian Freud, when, his cheek eaten through by cancer, he finally asked his doctor for a pain-killer, on the grounds that "it is only torture now and no longer has any sense". In both these cases the freedom of the choosing will is absent, and so, therefore, are the satisfaction, and sense of mastery and closure, which genuine philosophical resignation ought to confer. There are times when it might be wisest to avert one's gaze, and foolish to wish to confront the truth at any price.

The poets are broadly split between depicting the horrors of old age (Larkin) and celebrating (not quite like Cicero) its dignity, utility and place in the grand scheme of things (Wordsworth). It seems unrealistic to praise one view and damn the other. For each seems to capture a truth, even though their accounts – or perhaps rather their emphases – conflict. Then there is Yeats, torn between the ferocious egoistic posturing that had always been part of his character and a mature realization of the real and tragic ambivalences inherent in old age. Let us look at him first.

Yeats

The muscle-bound, would-be heroic Yeats is familiar enough, and goes down well with some (often Irish) readers:

Grant me an old man's frenzy,
Myself must I remake
Till I am Timon and Lear
Or that William Blake
Who beat upon the wall
Till Truth obeyed his call;
A mind Michael Angelo knew
That can pierce the clouds,
Or inspired by frenzy
Shake the dead in their shrouds;
Forgotten else by mankind,
An old man's eagle mind.[253]

George Orwell acutely noted the inexpressible affectation of the "that" before "William Blake". But here is a far more searching self-portrait (the speaker, beyond doubt, being the poet himself):

An aged man is but a paltry thing,
A tattered coat upon a stick, unless
Soul clap its hands and sing, and louder sing
For every tatter in its mortal dress,
Nor is there singing school but studying
Monuments of its own magnificence;
And therefore I have sailed the seas and come
To the holy city of Byzantium.[254]

The target here is surely the "heroic" Yeats, and all this high-toned spiritual bombast ("soul", "monuments", "magnificence", etc.) is seen precisely as an enforced compensation ("louder sing / For every tatter in its mortal dress") for the physical humiliations of age ("a paltry thing"). In the last stanza of the poem the speaker satirically voices what must be the oddest ambition ever in an old person, to become one of a collection of mechanical songbirds, which Yeats had read, in Gibbon and elsewhere, that a Byzantine Emperor once possessed:

Once out of nature I shall never take
My bodily form from any natural thing,
But such a form as Grecian goldsmiths make
Of hammered gold and gold enamelling

162

To keep a drowsy Emperor awake;
Or set upon a golden bough to sing
To lords and ladies of Byzantium
Of what is past, or passing, or to come.

Rhetorically impressive those lines may be, but it is astonishing how frequently their self-directed irony has been missed. Anyone in doubt need only compare them with the real singing birds, evocative of the "sensual music" of youth, in the poem's opening stanza; though there youth too is ironically observed, being in its own way as blinkered as age. *Si jeunesse savait, si vieillesse pouvait.* Moreover, men being vain and silly like both the original King Lear and Yeats's Lear in "An Acre of Grass", old age's lack of *pouvoir* is just what leads to its lack of *savoir.* Far preferable is the Nobel Laureate, Senator Yeats of "Among School Children", on a visit to a primary school:

The children's eyes
In momentary wonder stare upon
A sixty-year-old smiling public man.[255]

No use trying that "old man's eagle mind" stuff on them, then (the key word is "momentary"). And, remembering his youthful infatuation with Maud Gonne (as beautiful as Helen of Troy, daughter of Leda), the poet is moved to vanity, but checks himself:

And I though never of Ledaean kind
Had pretty plumage once – enough of that,
Better to smile on all that smile, and show
There is a comfortable kind of old scarecrow.[256]

Most of us would happily settle for as much self-deprecating dignity as that. Better to be a comfortable old scarecrow than a paltry one, and much better, surely, than to be a feathered, twittering musical box.

Larkin

Philip Larkin's poetry about old age – an age he himself never reached – is almost unrelievedly bleak, and many dislike it. But who can deny its truth as far as it goes; that is, even though it may not be the whole story? Here he is, at his most brutally realistic, on senility. The scene is presumably a nursing home that the speaker (again, obviously the poet) is visiting, the diametric opposite of Yeats's schoolroom:

> *What do they think has happened, the old fools,*
> *To make them like this? Do they somehow suppose*
> *It's more grown-up when your mouth hangs open and drools,*
> *And you keep on pissing yourself, and can't remember*
> *Who called this morning? Or that, if they only chose,*
> *They could alter things back to when they danced all night,*
> *Or went to their wedding, or sloped arms some September?*
> *Or do they fancy there's really been no change,*
> *And they've always behaved as if they were crippled or tight,*
> *Or sat through days of thin continuous dreaming*
> *Watching light move? If they don't (and they can't), it's strange:*
> *Why aren't they screaming?*[257]

As for the consolations of philosophy (Epicurus, Lucretius, *et al*, including Cicero):

> *At death, you break up: the bits that were you*
> *Start speeding away from each other for ever*
> *With no one to see. It's only oblivion, true:*
> *We had it before, but then it was going to end,*
> *And was all the time merging with a unique endeavour*
> *To bring to bloom the million-petalled flower*
> *Of being there. Next time you can't pretend*
> *There'll be anything else. And these are the first signs:*
> *Not knowing how, not hearing who, the power*
> *Of choosing gone. Their looks show that they're for it:*
> *Ash hair, toad hands, prune face dried into lines –*
> *How can they ignore it?*[258]

And, bringing the situation back to himself personally, here he is at his grimmest and most explicit, in "Aubade":

> *I work all day, and get half drunk at night.*
> *Waking at four to soundless dark, I stare.*

In time the curtain edges will grow light.
Till then I see what's really always there:
Unresting death, a whole day nearer now,
Making all thought impossible but how
And where and when I shall myself die.
Arid interrogation: yet the dread
Of dying, and being dead,
Flashes afresh to hold and horrify.

The mind blanks at the glare. Not in remorse
– The good not used, the love not given, time
Torn off unused – nor wretchedly because
An only life can take so long to climb
Clear of its wrong beginnings, and may never:
But at the total emptiness forever,
The sure extinction that we travel to
And shall be lost in always. Not to be here,
Not to be anywhere,
And soon; nothing more terrible, nothing more true.

This is a special way of being afraid
No trick dispels. Religion used to try,
That vast moth-eaten musical brocade
Created to pretend we never die,
And specious stuff that says No rational being
Can fear a thing it cannot feel, not seeing
That this is what we fear – no sight, no sound,
No touch or taste or smell, nothing to think with,
Nothing to love or link with,
The anaesthetic from which none come round.[259]

What is it that led Lucretius to accept that "specious stuff" from Epicurus – which is not, in truth, so very foolish – and Larkin not to? (I say nothing of religion.) Perhaps, as Plato and Cicero said, these things are determined by character, or are simply visceral, beyond argument. Here, after a fourth stanza, is Larkin's conclusion:

Slowly light strengthens, and the room takes shape.
It stands plain as a wardrobe, what we know,

Have always known, know that we can't escape
Yet can't accept. One side will have to go.
Meanwhile telephones crouch, getting ready to ring
In locked-up offices, and all the uncaring
Intricate rented world begins to rouse.
The sky is white as clay, with no sun.
Work has to be done.
Postmen like doctors go from house to house.

All that remains is a different kind of anaesthetic or blanking out: the routines of the workaday world in which, graphically, telephones "crouch" (they were curved in those days), getting ready to *spring* into action (namely to *ring*), and where, with blithe unconcern, as in another fear-of-death poem "The Building" (a hospital, never so named), "girls with hair-dos fetch / Their separates from the cleaners". There are, however, rare moments, the more compelling for their rarity, which come as an immense relief, in which Larkin, though evidently little disposed that way, and therefore unsentimentally, realizes that "What will survive of us is love" ("An Arundel Tomb") or that "we should be careful / Of each other, we should be kind / While there is still time" ("The Mower", a brilliant allusion to Marvell's "Mower" pastorals and the traditional Grim Reaper, the mower here being merely the poet's lawnmower, and its hapless victim a hedgehog he had once fed).

Wordsworth

Finally, Wordsworth. Here is the last two-thirds of his "Old Man Travelling: Animal Tranquillity and Decay", with its deceptively dead-pan ending, at once consolatory, poignant and shocking:

He is insensibly subdued
To settled quiet: he is one by whom
All effort seems forgotten, one to whom
Long patience has such mild composure given,
That patience now doth seem a thing, of which
He hath no need. He is by nature led
To peace so perfect, that the young behold

With envy, what the old man hardly feels.
– I asked him whither he was bound, and what
The object of his journey; he replied
"Sir! I am going many miles to take
A last leave of my son, a mariner,
Who from a sea-fight has been brought to Falmouth,
And there is dying in an hospital." [260]

The implication is that if he can endure such things, so can we. The old man's passive acceptance of his lot, indeed his near-insensibility to it, is tied up with his decrepitude and represents that almost as a providential blessing, at the same time appearing to play down what must surely be a genuine, objective occasion for a grief and concern which he himself barely feels, so that his situation, though deserving of it, makes little or no direct claim on our sympathy, which thus, though real, is denied an outlet.

Another poem which cannot but shock modern sensibilities is Wordsworth's "The Old Cumberland Beggar", in which the old man's silence, solitude, weariness and absolute poverty are justified (yes, *justified*) by the charitable impulses they excite among the rural poor, who take pleasure in supporting him from their own scanty store, and whose charity is passed down in turn through him to the birds, to whom he feeds his crumbs. "Deem not this man useless!", says the poet to the politicians – "ye / Who are so restless in your wisdom, ye / Who have a broom still ready in your hands / To rid the world of nuisances" – and who, if they had their way, would send the old man to the workhouse. (A note by Wordsworth adds that "the political economists were about that time beginning the war on mendicity in all its forms, and, by implication if not directly, on almsgiving also".) And of course the courteous, uncomplaining old leech-gatherer in "Resolution and Independence" is a lesson in fortitude to the poet himself, full as he is of brooding melancholy and self-pity, and also impelled to extend to the old man a pity he might seem to deserve, but which he does not feel for himself and does not seek from others.

Finally, there is the heart-wrenching tale of the old shepherd, "Michael", who, having increased his substance by a lifetime's industry, loses half to ill-luck, and sends his only child Luke, the son of his old age, away to "the dissolute city" to repair their fortunes. There the boy falls into "evil courses" and is forced to flee the country. Michael is left to complete the sheepfold they had begun together as a kind of covenant between them:

There is a comfort in the strength of love;
'Twill make a thing endurable, which else
Would overset the brain, or break the heart:
I have conversed with more than one who well
Remember the old man, and what he was
Years after he had heard this heavy news.
His bodily frame had been from youth to age
Of an unusual strength. Among the rocks
He went, and still looked up to sun and cloud,
And listened to the wind; and, as before,
Performed all kinds of labour for his sheep,
And for the land, his small inheritance.
And to that hollow dell from time to time
Did he repair, to build the fold of which
His flock had need. 'Tis not forgotten yet
The pity which was then in every heart
For the old man – and 'tis believed by all
That many and many a day he thither went,
And never lifted up a single stone.

Of course, because there now is no one to inherit. Wordsworth, though famously devoid of ironic sophistication, seems to me one of the profoundest writers on the subject of old age who have ever lived.

What, however, of the official literature? If it is not remarkable for profound wisdom, that is no great matter. The most basic advice is that which must apply to all cases, and I have observed that "old age" is as various as those subject to it. For most people old age is sufficiently a problem for them either to wish not to think about it (like Larkin), or to accept and to plan for it (like Cicero's Cato). Which of these is the more rational course will presumably depend on how firm one's expectations are both of reaching old age, and of the particular old age one expects. But clearly old age is a lot more fulfilling (or bearable) when free from disease, poverty and pointlessness, and a great deal of popular counsel, in books (I have one in front of me now), medical and financial pamphlets and the press, is modestly, and very sensibly, devoted to suggesting how to minimize those things or their effects.

This is surely more rational, not than moral exhortations as to how to rise above them (for one may still have to do so), but than *beginning* with such exhortations. To start on the ground rather than in the empyrean is consistent, as I have shown, with the so-called wisdom of antiquity, much of which, over and above the moralizing, is simple good sense and sound practical advice similar to ours. There is a science of geriatrics, but as yet there seems not to be any bogus "expertise" about old age, as there is, say, about child-rearing, or education (or crime, and much else), I suppose because we oldsters are beyond indoctrination and cannot usefully be conscripted into the exciting new future which our masters have in store for younger generations. So for that, at least, we should be grateful. Old age is troublesome enough as it is.

CHAPTER 11

Being ill

Carolyn and David Womersley

Knowledge comes, wisdom lingers.
TENNYSON "LOCKSLEY HALL"

The great fear

Nobody wants to be ill, and when one does fall ill, the physical or psychological symptoms make it perfectly natural to wish to be rid of the illness as soon as possible. It is also the case that certain kinds of behaviour dispose those who practise it towards certain illnesses (for instance, smoking disposes towards lung cancer). It therefore may be sensible to avoid certain activities if you wish to reduce your likelihood of contracting the diseases to which they seem to lead (although the prudent will not always be guided by the most recent medical advice on these issues – consider how that advice has shifted over recent years in relation to say, diet and alcohol – and will always wish to balance traditional wisdom against modern opinion).

But, although illness undoubtedly brings with it suffering, and although epidemiology tells us that, to a certain extent, we may put ourselves in the way of illness or not as we choose, the twin unspoken premises on which so many current attitudes towards illness are based – namely, that it is an unmitigated evil, and that it can be kept at bay indefinitely – are not only both false, but have also the malign effect of weakening us before the (inevitable) advent of illness

Wisdom teaches that illness cannot be indefinitely postponed and is not an unmitigated evil

These premises remain unspoken because, when stated, their

questionableness and even absurdity are immediately apparent. Nevertheless, they guide many modern attitudes towards health – attitudes which are fuelled more by the desire at whatever cost to fend off death and unnaturally to prolong physical youth than by an understanding that what constitutes health changes as one moves through the various stages of life. It is an outlook on illness encapsulated by an initially amusing but finally depressing quip from Woody Allen. When reassured that his work as a film-maker would make him immortal, Allen replied that he would prefer to be immortal by never dying. It is a natural response, but only a little reflection is needed to see that someone who lives their life on this basis has, in the deepest sense, never really been alive at all. This is the paradox of modernity's great fear of death. By placing so extravagant a value upon mere life, it impoverishes what it claims to prize. By the same token, modern attitudes towards illness reveal, in those who espouse them, a mistaken attitude towards life – an attitude which misunderstands why life is valuable, and which in a puerile spirit of imbecillity wishes to re-negotiate or resile from the conditions upon which alone we can enjoy life. As Sydney Smith said with amused contempt in his final illness,

> I am now...taking all proper care of myself, which care consists in eating nothing that I like and doing nothing that I wish.[261]

There are worse things than death

People's thoughts about illness were not always paralysed and narrowed by our base fear of death. Older societies knew well that many worse things could happen to you than to die ("*Malo mori quam foedari*"). They knew, too, that illness, as the herald of death, nevertheless brought with it gifts and opportunities, provided it was approached in the correct manner. The advocates of modernity may scoff that older societies were condemned to stoicism and to the search for fugitive goods in what we instinctively feel to be the absolute evil of disease, because their medical expertise was so rudimentary. Certainly, it would be an awful thing (for instance) to have to undergo an operation without an anaesthetic. But our contention here is not to dismiss the undoubted advances in medical technique which have occurred since the early nineteenth century. Still less is it to belittle or dismiss the many benefits which have flowed from the fact that doctors now have at their disposal a much wider range of treatments and procedures than did their predecessors. Rather it is gently to insist once more upon the value of those older attitudes towards illness which have been smothered by modern medicine's hubristic reliance upon mere technical expertise.

Towards the end of *Brideshead Revisited*, with Lord Marchmain at the point of death, Charles Ryder buttonholes the doctor who has just visited:

> *I said to the doctor, who was with us daily: "He's got a wonderful will to live hasn't he?"*

> *"Would you put it like that? I should say a great fear of death."*

> *"Is there a difference?"*

> *"Oh dear, yes. He doesn't derive any strength from his fear, you know. It's wearing him out."*[262]

This is not just an exchange between two characters. It is an exchange between the modern outlook of shallow irreverence and incomprehension embodied by Charles, and a more traditional and morally subtle wisdom to which Waugh's doctor gives voice.

Our current predicaments and discontents on how we meet the illness which, at some time, will touch every life, can be encapsulated in two, interconnected observations. Today, virtually all patients are as morally illiterate as Charles, and can see no difference between the will to live and the fear of death. At the same time, changes within the medical profession – changes partly self-inflicted, partly responses to the attitudes of the patients whom they are increasingly encouraged to regard as consumers in what is essentially a commercial relationship – have all but eradicated the kind of doctor whom Waugh imagined in *Brideshead*. The encounter between doctor and patient today is too often a meeting between querulous petulance, and an over-academic peddler of "cures".

In a sense, the two parties are well-matched, since modern patients, for the most part, prefer to be supplied with the fixes which such doctors provide. The insights supplied by wisdom take too much thinking about, and in any case often whisper what today's patients don't want to hear – that they will surely die, that while individual ailments may be relieved, in the end all medicine is palliative, and that disease is the harbinger of death even when death does not immediately ensue. This, however, is explicitly what Hezekiah was told by Isaiah:

> *In those days was Hezekiah sick unto death. And the prophet Isaiah the son of Amos came to him, and said unto him, Thus saith the Lord, set thine house in order; for thou shalt die, and not live.*[263]

How to be a patient

It is characteristic of children to be impatient, especially of what crosses them. Modern medicine has infantilised patients by encouraging the expectation that treatments will, thanks to technological or pharmacological expertise, produce a swift and immediate cure. Occasionally (even, often) it can satisfy this expectation. But eventually it will fail, and when it does so, its patients will be left bewildered, unguided and angry: indeed, like children. Older attitudes towards disease were much wiser on this score. Because they were aware that illness possesses a moral as well as a physical dimension, they also taught that it might not be sane to pursue a cure at any cost. In *All's Well That Ends Well*, the King is properly and healthily cautious about trusting Helena when she arrives at court promising to cure his fistula:

> *We thank you maiden,*
> *But may not be so credulous of cure,*
> *When our most learned doctors leave us, and*
> *The congregated College have concluded*
> *That labouring art can never ransom nature*
> *From her unaidable estate. I say we must not*
> *So stain our judgement or corrupt our hope,*
> *To prostitute our past-cure malady*
> *To empirics, or to dissever so*
> *Our great self and our credit, to esteem*
> *A senseless help, when help past sense we deem.*[264]

The narrow and indeflectible pursuit of cure is indeed a corruption of hope. It is based on an incomplete understanding of disease, and is condemned to be finally unavailing. A contemporary of Shakespeare's,

John Donne, understood this well:

> *To cure the sharpe accidents of diseases, is a great worke; to cure the disease it selfe, is a greater; but to cure the body, the root, the occasion of diseases, is a worke reserved for the great Physitian, which he doth never any other way, but by glorifying these bodies in the next world.*[265]

Donne does not belittle the work of physical cure, but he sees clearly that it is not the whole story of disease. And indeed, *Devotions Upon Emergent Occasions* is the greatest work in English about what it is to be ill. Written during Donne's convalescence from a serious illness (possibly typhus) which had brought him to the point of death in the winter of 1623, it teems with insights which are pertinent even to those who do not share the religious consolations which allow its author eventually to repose in the comfortable notion of a "great Physitian".

In the "First Meditation" Donne affects to write from the uneducated standpoint of natural instinct, in which all human efforts are directed towards attaining and maintaining somatic health, and in which disease consequently arrives as a monstrous and unheralded intrusion:

> *We study Health, and we deliberate upon our meats, and drink, and Ayre, and exercises, and we hew and wee polish every stone, that goes to that building [ie the body]; and so our Health is a long & a regular work; But in a minute a Cannon batters all, overthrowes all, demolishes all; a Sicknes unprevented for all our diligence, unsuspected for all our curiositie; nay, undeserved, if we consider only disorder, summons us, seizes us, possesses us, destroyes us in an instant.*[266]

But as his illness takes its course, Donne is gradually educated out of such understandable, but ultimately only beguiling, attitudes. In the first place, he becomes aware of the error of placing all your confidence in physicians:

> *Thou who sendes us for a blessing to the Phisician, doest not make it a curse to us, to go, when thou sendest. Is not the curse rather in this, that onely hee falls into the hands of the Phisician, that casts himself wholy, intirely upon the Phisician, confides in him, relies upon him, attends all from him, and neglects that spirituall phisicke, which thou also hast instituted in thy Church: so to fall into the hands of the Phisician, is a*

175

sinne, and a punishment of former sinnes; so, as Asa fell, who in his disease, sought not to the Lord, but to the Phisician.[267]

Donne's religious faith is instrumental in his articulation of this idea, but his essential insight – that to cast yourself wholly and entirely upon the doctors is a false haven – is one which even those without religious faith can endorse, provided they are not trapped within the pale of materialist hedonism, and are therefore able to recognize goods above mere gratification.

Donne then goes on to explore the moral aspect of sickness. Perhaps surprisingly, he does not find pain to be the most distressing aspect of being ill:

As Sicknesse is the greatest misery, so the greatest misery of sicknes is solitude; when the infectiousnes of the disease deterrs them who should assist, from coming; Even the Phisician dares scarse come. Solitude is a torment, which is not threatned in hell it selfe.[268]

This is not just a physical solitude: it is also a moral estrangement. So Donne prays for what he calls "conformable affections", by which he means a moral solidarity with the rest of humanity:

Give me tender, and supple, and conformable affections, that as I joy with them that joy, and mourne with them, that mourne, so I may feare with them that feare. And since thou hast vouchsafed to discover to me, in his feare whom thou hast admitted to be my assistance, in this sicknesse, that there is danger therein, let me not, O Lord, go about to overcome the sense of that fear, so far, as to pretermit the fitting, and preparing of my selfe, for the worst that may be feard, the passage out of this life.[269]

It is striking that, in Donne's mind, this moral solidarity is so closely associated with the proper preparation for death. But from our familiarity with the blandishments of modern "expertise" medicine, we can see why this must be so. By distracting us from the truth that, eventually and inevitably, its remedies will fail, "expertise" medicine makes it harder for us to prepare properly for death. In so doing, it erodes our "conformable affections" by implicitly encouraging us in the delusion that, in our case, the common fate of humanity can certainly be postponed, perhaps even suspended indefinitely.

But even if the implicit promises of "expertise" medicine were not dangerous delusions, even if they could be made good, would we be wise to avail ourselves of them? In Book Three of *Gulliver's Travels*, Gulliver visits the island of Luggnagg, whose inhabitants have been freed from the fear of death as the greatest evil by the experience of living alongside the "Struldbruggs", rare offspring distinguished from birth by "a red circular Spot in the Forehead...which was an infallible Mark that it should never dye". Gulliver is at first moved to rapture by the news of these (as he thinks) favoured beings:

> *Happy Nation, where every Child has at least a Chance for being immortal! Happy People who enjoy so many living Examples of antient Virtue, and have Masters ready to instruct them in the Wisdom of all former Ages!*

He could not be more wrong. The Struldbruggs are miserable outcasts, "espised and hated by all Sorts of People". True, they do not enjoy eternal youth, only eternal life. But what is most appalling about their condition is not their physical decrepitude, so much as their separation from the common sequences and successions of human life. Illness has its place in those sequences and successions, and the experience of illness is an important element in the experience of being human.

Illness as a moral education

Illness provides the patient with a chance to develop and strengthen a whole array of moral virtues: courage, forbearance, patience (of course), selflessness, a determination not to surrender to pointless fretting. In 1783 Johnson was

> *seized with a spasmodick asthma of such violence, that he was confined to the house in great pain, being sometimes obliged to sit all night in his chair, a recumbent posture being so hurtful to his respiration, that he could not endure lying in bed; and there came upon him at the same time that oppressive and fatal disease, a dropsy. It was a very severe winter, which probably aggravated his complaints; and the solitude in which Mr. Levett and Mrs. Williams had left him, rendered his life very gloomy.*

However, Johnson did not crumple under this complicated adversity:

> He…had none of that unsocial shyness which we commonly see in people afflicted with sickness. He did not hide his head from the world, in solitary abstraction; he did not deny himself to the visits of his friends and acquaintances; but at all times, when he was not overcome by sleep, was ready for conversation as in his best days.[270]

A bout of sickness can also allow others to demonstrate similar fortitude and compassion. For instance, the illness which laid Tennyson low in 1888 elicited letters from Jowett and Browning which do great honour to the writers, the subject and the recipients. The first was written by Jowett to Lady Tennyson:

> I am afraid that you must be in great anxiety but not without hope. May God strengthen and help you! I believe that the patient may at all times minister to himself if he is conscious, and that that strong frame and mind will not be easily overcome in its struggle. Give my love to him and tell him that I hope that he is at rest, knowing that we are all in the hands of God. I would have him think sometimes that no one has done more for mankind in our own time, having found expression for their noblest thoughts and having never written a line that he would wish to blot; and that this benefit, which he has conferred on the English language and people, will be an everlasting possession to them, as great as any poet has ever given to any nation, and that those who have been his friends will always think of him with love and admiration, and speak to others of the honour of having known him. He who has such record of life should have the comfort of it in the late years of it: there may be some things which he blames, and some which he laments, but as a whole he has led a true and noble life, and he need not trouble himself about small matters.

The second was written by Browning to the poet himself:

> I was at Venice when the first news of your illness reached me, and I hardly know how I could resist so long the impulse I at last gave way to, that of inquiring directly how you are. Probably it came of needing only to know this more exactly than was possible by the indirect means in my power, for as to any object beyond it, I know that, being what you

are, there is no need to put in evidence the thorough love that I have always had for yourself, no less than my absolute admiration of your work. The circumstances of life never seemed to permit me a neighbourhood, and intercourse, which would have been a more valued honour and gratifying privilege than, with one exception, ever befell me, still I could have taken observation of the star beyond an actual reach which would have made me happy indeed: all which, I repeat, you know and must have long known; and it is only now that I trouble you with the telling, because the last accounts I have heard of your condition are favourable, and one's breath naturally ceases to be held when the danger is, if God please, over: and mine relieves itself, and you will forgive if it in any way importunes you: that it should not do so is all I desire.[271]

But the moral and emotional opportunities which made possible sentiments of this refinement, comfort, delicacy and strength are not available within an outlook on illness which sees it as a purely somatic event, ánd hence an unqualified evil.

Why unreasonable patients get the doctors they deserve

What do we want a doctor to be? A possible model is one of the fantasies of James Thurber's famous creation, Walter Mitty. Driving past the hospital, Mitty's imagination is launched. The "millionaire banker" Wellington McMillan is undergoing an operation for a particularly difficult case of "obstreosis of the ductal tract". Mitty has been asked to assist Drs Renshaw and Benbow and the specialists Remington and Pritchard-Mitford, when suddenly:

A huge complicated machine, connected to the operating table, with many tubes and wires, began at this moment to go pocketa-pocketa-pocketa. "The new anaesthetizer is giving way!" shouted an interne. "There is no one in the East who knows how to fix it!" "Quiet, man!" said Mitty, in a low, cool voice. He sprang to the machine, which was now going pocketa-pocketa-queep-pocketa-queep. He began fingering delicately a row of glistening dials. "Give me a fountain-pen!" he snapped. Someone handed him a fountain pen. He pulled a faulty piston out of the machine and inserted the pen in its place. "That will hold it for ten minutes," he said. "Get on with the operation." A nurse hurried over and whispered to Renshaw, and Mitty saw the man turn pale. "Coreopsis has set in," said Renshaw nervously. "If you would take over, Mitty?" Mitty looked at him and at the craven figure of Benbow, who drank, and at the grave, uncertain faces of the two great specialists. "If you wish," he said.[272]

Of course, there is no mention made of the patient in any of this. This is medicine as vainglorious ostentation, a display of expertise on either malfunctioning bodies or malfunctioning machines. What Thurber offered as a self-evident, and therefore funny, fantasy of a puerile inadequate is, however, increasingly how the immaturity of modern patients is encouraging doctors to be. The rise in litigation aimed at doctors shows how easily patients can come bitterly to resent those to whom they look for cures when those cures either go wrong or are not forthcoming. What is not so immediately apparent is that this readiness to sue is what you are left with when the unreasonable desire that, in all cases, medical expertise can make a problem "go away" is disappointed. It is best regarded as curdled credulity. Confronted by such patients, natural self-interest pushes doctors towards "quick-fix" medicine, even when that may not be either feasible or in the patient's own best long-term interests. Anything rather than not comply with a patient's demands, no matter how unreasonable. The business of patient education takes too long, the emotions standing in the way of understanding in the minds of those who can imagine nothing better than an eternity of somatic vigour are in any case too powerful. And this gain in "expertise" tends to be purchased at the expense of wisdom, since (as T S Eliot appreciated) the former naturally drives out the latter:

> *It is perhaps too much to expect of any man to possess both specialised scientific power and wisdom [especially since] wisdom seems to be a commodity less and less available in educational institutions; for the methods and ideals coming into vogue in modern education...are not calculated to cultivate a disposition towards wisdom.*[273]

A poem written by Dr Johnson, "On the Death of Dr Robert Levet", offers us a different idea of what a doctor might be. Robert Levet (1705-82) was a poor physician who lodged with Johnson. By all accounts Johnson could be rather abrupt with Levet, while he was alive. But when he died, he commemorated his virtues in a poem which demonstrates how well Johnson understood, both what doctors can and should do, and what this particular doctor had done. Here are the poem's central stanzas:

> *Well tried through many a varying year,*
> *See LEVET to the grave descend;*
> *Officious, innocent, sincere,*
> *Of ev'ry friendless name the friend.*
> *Yet still he fills affection's eye,*
> *Obscurely wise, and coarsely kind;*
> *Nor, letter'd arrogance, deny*
> *Thy praise to merit unrefin'd.*
> *When fainting nature call'd for aid,*
> *And hov'ring death prepar'd the blow,*
> *His vig'rous remedy display'd*
> *The power of art without the show.*
> *In misery's darkest caverns known,*
> *His useful care was ever nigh,*
> *Where hopeless anguish pour'd his groan,*
> *And lonely want retir'd to die.*
> *No summons mock'd by chill delay,*
> *No petty gain disdain'd by pride,*
> *The modest wants of ev'ry day*
> *The toil of ev'ry day supplied.*

Some of Johnson's vocabulary here has shifted in meaning since the poem was composed (for instance, in Johnson's day "officious" meant simply "dutiful", without any pejorative connotation). Nevertheless, two insights in particular emerge from Johnson's epitaph for Levet. The first is that medicine should be practised in a way which is modestly self-effacing, rather than ostentatious – this is why Levet embodied the "power of art without the show". The second is that this modesty is fitting, because all medicine is in the end palliative. In the end, doctors have to forsake the lure of the vainglorious remedy, and accept instead that they must mitigate the inevitable. So Levet ministered to "hopeless anguish", knowing that supplying an immediate cure is but one aspect, and perhaps not the most important, of a doctor's duties.

Johnson contrasted Levet's useful virtues to what he called "lettered arrogance". The ascendancy of "expertise" medicine has led to something akin to "lettered arrogance" establishing itself within medical education. It used to be the case that the academic qualifications needed to enter medical school in this country were not overwhelmingly high. The reason for this was not cronyism or the old boy network, as was commonly claimed. It was rather that those who ran our medical schools then recognised that narrow academic ability was not the prime requisite for a doctor, except perhaps for those very few who would hope to work on the very cutting edge of medical research. Broader human and moral qualities would be much more important, particularly for a general practitioner, who hardly ever encounters a problem which is so medically recondite that the kind of training needed to produce superlative academic qualifications is at all useful.

However, the increasing insistence on the very highest academic qualifications for entry to medical school is gradually producing a new breed of doctor: academic, narrow, in human terms brittle, and having imbibed an incomplete notion of what it is to be a doctor. The ethical and even literary components in medical education which some medical schools are now incorporating into their syllabuses indicate an awareness of this problem, although they themselves are initiatives on too small a scale greatly to affect the problem. What we need is that the populace at large should be re-educated about illness. However, it is difficult to see the rising cohort of doctors taking the lead in that task, since they have been trained up in a system which has increasingly had at its heart an image of what it is to be a doctor which is complicit with, and indeed produced by, those attitudes towards disease amongst patients which need to be remedied. It looks, then, as if it will have to be a case of "Patient, cure thyself".

CHAPTER 12

Dying

Peter Mullen

The words of the great traditions in religion, the inspired verses of the best poets from many cultures and civilizations and the profound contemplation of the most creative philosophers should not merely be described as "noble", "tender", "uplifting" etc. What these words do is actually to instil and create in us what is noble, what is courageous and what is tender. It is not so much that the words are, say, uplifting, but that we are actually uplifted by hearing or reading them. These great words produce psychological and spiritual change in us for the good, for our good.

Consider death and resurrection, the Christian Hope as expressed in the Bible and the *Book of Common Prayer.*

> *The Lord is my shepherd; I shall not want. He maketh me to lie down in green pastures: he leadeth me beside the still waters. He restoreth my soul: he leadeth me in the paths of righteousness for his name's sake. Yea, though I walk through the valley of the shadow of death, I will fear no evil: for thou art with me; thy rod and thy staff they comfort me.*[274]

This passage succeeds because it is not about comfort in the abstract. It mentions real things – things with which we are familiar in the world: green pastures, still waters, rod and staff. The same is true of this next quotation, only even more so. It too is about real things. The wonder is that these are unpleasant things: worms devouring the corpse etc, but in the hands of the religious genius who wrote them, even these unpleasant things are turned to provide hope and encouragement. So worms will destroy my body. It doesn't matter, for God will redeem even that catastrophe.

I know that my Redeemer liveth, and that he shall stand at the latter day upon the earth. And though after my skin worms destroy this body, yet in my flesh shall I see God: Whom I shall see for myself, and mine eyes shall behold, and not another.[275]

God so loved the world that he gave his only begotten Son that whosoever believeth in him should not perish, but have everlasting life.[276]

I am the resurrection and the life, saith the Lord: he that believeth in me, though he were dead, yet shall he live: And whosoever liveth and believeth in me shall never die.[277]

The next extract shows how the rhythms of a piece of prose are also part of its meaning and its effect. It is a poetic image of the Good Shepherd who goes before his sheep, finds the best place for them and then returns to take them to it. It is above all intimately pastoral.

Let not your heart be troubled: ye believe in God, believe also in me. In my Father's house are many mansions: if it were not so, I would have told you. I go to prepare a place for you. And if I go and prepare a place for you, I will come again and receive you unto myself; that where I am, there ye may be also.[278]

In the following verses St Paul uses the rhetoric of oratory to inspire us with God's consolation. The very building up, as it were layer upon layer, of those awful things – death, life, powers and principalities, peril, nakedness and the sword, turns the words with which he ends – the love of God in Christ Jesus – into a triumph of emphasis. All those terrible things which we fear might separate us from the love of God are not able to do so.

Who shall separate us from the love of Christ? Shall tribulation, or distress, or persecution, or famine, or nakedness, or peril, or sword? As it is written, For thy sake we are killed all the day long; we are accounted as sheep for the slaughter. Nay, in all these things we are more than conquerors through him that loved us. For I am persuaded, that neither death, nor life, nor angels, nor principalities, nor powers, nor things present, nor things to come, Nor height, nor depth, nor any other creature, shall be able to separate us from the love of God, which is in Christ Jesus our Lord.[279]

The following is part of the lesson set for The Burial of the Dead. It rings out with amazing confidence in the very presence of the corpse

If in this life only we have hope in Christ, we are of all men most miserable. But now is Christ risen from the dead, and become the first-fruits of them that slept. For since by man came death, by man came also the resurrection of the dead. For as in Adam all die, even so in Christ shall all be made alive.[280]

Sometimes St Paul uses argument to great effect, as in the next quotation. And his scathing, sarcastic dismissal of the sceptic – "Thou fool!" – is thrilling. Also the style – stating one thing and then its opposite over and over again – parallelism – gives depth to the argument because it is itself an example of the argument's conclusion: the bad things are replaced by what is good.

But some man will say, How are the dead raised up? And with what body do they come? Thou fool, that which thou sowest, thou sowest not that body that shall be, but bare grain, it may chance of wheat, or of some other grain: But God giveth it a body as it hath pleased him, and to every seed his own body. All flesh is not the same flesh: but there is one kind of flesh of men, another flesh of beasts, and another of birds. There are also celestial bodies, and bodies terrestrial: but the glory of the celestial is one, and the glory of the terrestrial is another. There is one glory of the sun, and another glory of the moon, and another glory of the stars: for one star differeth from another star in glory. So also is the resurrection of the dead. It is sown in corruption; it is raised in incorruption: it is sown in dishonour; it is raised in glory: it is sown in weakness; it is raised in power: it is sown a natural body; it is raised a spiritual body. There is a natural body, and there is a spiritual body. And so it is written, The first man Adam was made a living soul; the last Adam was made a quickening spirit. Howbeit that was not first which is spiritual, but that which is natural; and afterward that which is spiritual. The first man is of the earth, earthy: the second man is the Lord from heaven. As is the earthy, such are they also that are earthy: and as is the heavenly, such are they also that are heavenly. And as we have borne the image of the earthy, we shall also bear the image of the heavenly. Now this I say, brethren, that flesh and blood cannot inherit the kingdom of God; neither doth corruption inherit incorruption. Behold, I shew you a mystery; We shall not all sleep, but we shall all be changed, In a moment, in the twinkling of an eye, at the last trump: for the trumpet shall sound, and the dead shall be raised incorruptible, and we shall be changed. For this corruptible must put on incorruption, and this mortal must put on immortality. So when this corruptible shall have put on incorruption, and this mortal shall have put on immortality, then shall be brought to pass the saying, Death is swallowed up in victory. O death, where is thy sting? O grave, where is thy victory? The sting of death is sin; and the strength of sin is the law. But thanks be to God, which giveth us the victory through our Lord Jesus Christ. [281]

Another word of comfort from St Paul:

But I would not have you to be ignorant, brethren, concerning them which are asleep, that ye sorrow not, even as others which have no hope. For if we believe that Jesus died and rose again, even so them also which sleep in Jesus will God bring with him. For this we say unto you by the word of the Lord, that we which are alive and remain unto the coming of the Lord shall not prevent them which are asleep. For the Lord himself shall descend from heaven with a shout, with the voice of the archangel, and with the trump of God: and the dead in Christ shall rise first: Then we which are alive and remain shall be caught up together with them in the clouds to meet the Lord in the air: and so shall we ever be with the Lord. Wherefore comfort one another with these words. [282]

And from the last book in the Bible

And I saw a new heaven and a new earth: for the first heaven and the first earth were passed away; and there was no more sea. And I John saw the holy city, new Jerusalem, coming down from God out of heaven, prepared as a bride adorned for her husband. And I heard a great voice out of heaven saying, Behold, the tabernacle of God is with men, and he will dwell with them, and they shall be his people, and God himself shall be with them, and be their God. And God shall wipe away all tears from their eyes; and there shall be no more death, neither sorrow, nor crying, neither shall there be any more pain: for the former things are passed away. [283]

Tenderness in a form

Here are some more extracts from Burial Services. Notice the extreme tenderness in that of 1549 in which the Minister actually addresses the deceased directly

Forasmuch as it hath pleased Almighty God of his great mercy to take unto himself the soul of our dear brother here departed, we therefore commit his body to the ground: earth to earth, ashes to ashes, dust to dust; in sure and certain hope of the Resurrection to eternal life, through our Lord Jesus Christ; who shall change our vile body, that it may be like unto his glorious body, according to the mighty working, whereby he is able to subdue all things to himself.[284]

I commend thy soul to God the Father Almighty, and thy body to the ground.[285]

I heard a voice from heaven, saying unto me, Write, From henceforth blessed are the dead which die in the Lord: even so saith the Spirit; for they rest from their labours.[286]

Come, ye blessed children of my Father, receive the kingdom prepared for you from the beginning of the world: Grant this, we beseech thee, O merciful Father, through Jesus Christ, our Mediator and Redeemer.[287]

Come to his assistance, ye saints of God, meet him, ye angels of the Lord, receiving his soul, offering it in the sight of the most high. May Christ who hast called thee, receive thee and may the angels conduct thee into Abraham's bosom Rest eternal grant unto him, O Lord, and let light perpetual shine upon him.[288]

O God, to whom it belongeth to have mercy and to spare, we humbly beseech thee for the soul of thy servant (handmaid) NAME whom you have summoned today from this world, that thou wouldst not deliver him into the hand of the enemy, nor forget him forever, but bid thine holy angels receive him to our home in Paradise, so that since he believed and hoped in Thee, he may not suffer the pains of hell but may possess eternal joys.[289]

May the angels lead thee into Paradise: may the martyrs receive thee at thy coming, and lead thee into the Holy City, Jerusalem. May the choir of angels receive thee, and with Lazarus, who once was poor, may thou go into eternal rest.[290]

Other themes

Less theological wisdom on death finds yet more themes; for instance, life as a task completed.

Every person has a particular mission which he is called upon to fulfil. When he has accomplished it, he is no longer needed on earth in the same form, and Providence uses him for something else. Mozart died at thirty-five; Raphael at practically the same age. Byron was only a little older. But each of them had accomplished his mission perfectly and it was time for them to go so that others still might have something left to do in a world created to last for a long while.[291]

More than one writer has noticed that death is not an experience for the living

So death, the most terrifying of ills, is nothing to us, since so long as we exist, death is not with us; but when death comes, then we do not exist. It does not then concern either the living or the dead, since for the former it is not, and the latter are no more.[292]

Death is not an event in life. Death is not lived through. If by eternity is understood not endless temporal duration but timelessness, then he lives eternally who lives in the present. Our life is endless in the way that our visual field is without limit. The temporal immortality of the human soul, that is, its eternal survival after death, is not only in no way guaranteed, but this assumption will not do for us what we have always tried to make it do. Is the riddle solved by the fact that I survive forever? Is this eternal life not as enigmatic as our present one?[293]

And since the man who is not feels no woe,
For death exempts him and wards off the blow

Which we, the living, only feel and bear;
What is there left for us in death to fear?
When once that pause of life has come between,
'Tis just the same as we had never been.[294]

"Suppose I guarantee you the continued existence of your individuality,
but on condition it is preceded by a completely unconscious death sleep
of ten thousand years."
"Yes, I would agree to that."
"But now, if after these ten thousand years have passed, it was forgotten
to wake you up, this would not I think be a very great misfortune, since
your period of non-being would have been so long compared with your
brief period of being, you would have got quite used to it. What is
certain, however, is that you would not have the least idea you had
failed to be woken up!"[295]

Death is most innocent: for when it is present, it hurts nobody; it is only
when it is absent that it troubles us.[296]

There was a time when we were not. This gives us no concern. Why
then should it trouble us that there will come a time when we shall
cease to be?[297]

We are not afraid to go to sleep, so why fear death?

Death be not proud, though some have called thee
Mighty and dreadful, for thou art not so,
For, those, whom thou thinkst thou dost overthrow,
Die not, poor death, nor yet canst thou kill me.
From rest and sleep, which but thy pictures be,
Much pleasure, then from thee, much more must flow,
And soonest our best men with thee do go,
Rest of their bones and soul's delivery.
Thou are slave to fate, chance, kings, and desperate men,
And dost with poison, war, and sickness dwell,
And poppy, or charms can make us sleep as well,
And better than thy stroke; why swellst thou then?
One short sleep past, we wake eternally,
And death shall be no more; death, thou shalt die.[298]

Death should not be regarded as an evil

It is impossible that anything so natural, so necessary, and so universal as death should ever have been designed by Providence as an evil to mankind.[299]

It is just as neurotic in old age not to focus on the goal of death as it is in youth to repress fantasies which have to do with the future.[300]

In death, the same unknown will appear as ever known to me. And, because I love this life, I know I shall love death as well. The child cries out when the mother takes away her right breast. In the next moment he finds in her left his consolation.[301]

*At the end you are left with the thought
That from Mozart to Siegfried Sassoon
All the people you respect
Are dead anyhow.*[302]

At ninety they lose their teeth and hair; they have at that age no distinction of taste, but eat and drink whatever they can get, without relish or appetite. The diseases they were subject to still continue. In talking, they forget the common names of things and of persons, even of those who are their nearest friends and relations. They never can amuse themselves with reading, because their memory will not carry them from the beginning of a sentence to its end. The reader will easily believe that from what I have learned on this subject, my keen appetite for perpetuity is much abated. I think no tyrant could invent a death into which I would not run with pleasure from such a life.[303]

Wisdom provides comfort for the bereaved

In thinking of all these virtues hold again, as it were, your son in your arms! He has now more leisure to devote to you. There is nothing now to call him away from you. Never again will he cause you anxiety, never again any grief. The only sorrow you could possibly have had from such a son so good is the sorrow you have had. All else is now exempt from the power of chance, and holds nothing but pleasure if only you know how to enjoy your son.[304]

Passionate grief does not link us with the dead, but cuts us off from them. It is just at those moments when I feel least sorrow – getting into my morning bath is one of them – that H. rushes upon my mind in her full reality, her otherness. Not, as in my worst moments, all foreshortened and patheticized by miseries, but as she is in her own right. This is good and tonic.[305]

If I should go before the rest of you
Break not a flower nor inscribe a stone,
Nor when I'm gone speak in a Sunday voice
But be the usual selves that I have known.
Weep if you must,
Parting is hell,
But life goes on,
So sing as well.[306]

I would rather sleep in the southern corner of a little country churchyard, than in the tomb of the Capulets. I should like, however, that my dust should mingle with kindred dust.[307]

Death is transcended by humour

I entered the Mummy Room at the British Museum under a vivid realisation of how the general resurrection might occur even as one stood among those solemn corpses turned into a sight for sightseers.[308]

Those who wish to abolish death, at what stage of life do they want the process to be halted? At the age of twenty. At thirty-five, in our prime? To be thirty-five for two years sounds attractive, certainly. But for three years? A little dull, surely. For five years – ridiculous. For ten – tragic. The sea and the stars and the wastes of the desert go on forever, and will not die. But the sea and the stars and the wastes of the desert are dead already.[309]

There are good reasons for believing in life after death

What reason do atheists have to say that one cannot rise from the dead? Which is the more difficult, to be born or to be reborn? That that which has never existed should exist, or that that which has existed should exist again? Is it more difficult to come into being than to return to it? Custom makes the one seem easy; absence of custom makes the other seem impossible: a vulgar way of judging![310]

Let the deepest elements in you disclose their deepest information. If there is nothing but non-being and oblivion waiting for us, the prevailing beliefs have not misled us, and that's that. This would astonish me, for the prevailing beliefs seldom satisfy my need for truth.[311]

In the end, it is how we live that matters most

It matters not how a man dies, but how he lives. The act of dying is not of importance, it lasts so short a time.[312]

Death and burial: how things used to be

Most deaths used to occur at home. The undertaker, usually a well-known and respected member of the local community, would be sent for as readily as the family doctor. As soon as the doctor had certified the death, the undertaker would wash and lay out the corpse and place it in its coffin. There was a tradition of viewing the body: friends and relations from near and far would come "to pay their respects".

Where I grew up, in a working-class industrial suburb of Leeds, the coffin was set out in the best room – usually called "the front room" – which also housed an upright piano (invariably out-of-tune) and an aspidistra (which had always "seen better days").

These front rooms were rarely used, except for laying-out. People did not have money to spare for coal for more than the living room fire. They might put a fire in the front room at Christmas or when it was some notable anniversary, such as a Silver Wedding. Consequently the room was usually rather damp, and the yellowing keys of the out-of-tune piano, overhung by the faded aspidistra, gave the place just the sort of genteel-dilapidated melancholy that suited the laying-out of Uncle Fred or Auntie Florrie.

The aspidistra, the piano and the coffin: nature, art and religion all in one room. The faintly musty smell and the quiet relieved only by the ticking of a clock which – though rarely did anyone consult it – was wound every day: another quasi-religious act. It was a powerful atmosphere in which to grow up and to receive one's first intimations of mortality. Dust and damp, nostalgic reminiscence and the solipsistic chiming of an unwatched clock. In such an atmosphere, you knew that death was, as Henry James said, "the distinguished thing".

The phrases spoken by attendant mourners were clichés, but clichés ennobled by sincerity of feeling and affection, and so elevated almost to the status of liturgy. They would say of the deceased, "She looks lovely"; "he's so peaceful". There were old music hall style jokes coined on these sombre little rituals: "By gum, Fred looks a lovely colour! That fortnight at Blackpool did him the world of good!" And laughing at these jokes became, in those old working-class communities, part of the ritual of mourning.

You were invited but not obliged to view the corpse. There was an etiquette about this as well, and it was one usually extended to children: "Do you want to look at your Auntie Florrie?" And, if the child did not so wish, then she was schooled to say, "No thank you. I'd rather remember her as she was".

Undertakers were "characters" who would often spin out comic-macabre stories about bodies who sat up and groaned (or performed other unmentionable minor acts) long after their decease had been certified. A local undertaker told me of how he had once been summoned to lay out an old girl of 93. When he arrived in her bedroom, he thought he noticed her blink an eye. Mere imagination, he said to himself. But then the old girl sat up and asked him to leave an extra pint of milk!

It was mysterious and it was scary, but it was real. The damp, the piano, the aspidistra and the clock gave it a context which, however worrying, meant that you had a way of putting death in perspective: the perspective was the shared life of the local community.

Our capacity to cope with metaphysical and spiritual problems, as with death and bereavement, is at least partly determined by the strength of local ties and all the informal rituals and jokes, superstitions and etiquette that create a folk-religion. Most truly felt religion is folk-religion. No one believed a word that the parson or the minister said at the funeral about life everlasting. What mattered was that the ritual of disposal was done rightly, that in the colloquial and powerful idiom, respects were paid. Uncle Fred, him dead. See him off with ham. It was a matter of pride bordering on liturgical exactitude that these things were done rightly and seen to be done well.

The inadequacy of modern funeral rites

Modern techniques for coping with dying, death and bereavement are inadequate. The *Book of Common Prayer* rang out its words of magnificent defiance:

> *I know that my Redeemer liveth, and that he shall stand upon the earth at the latter day, and though after my flesh worms destroy this body, yet in my flesh shall I see God.*

These are words of faith made more faithful by their association with the triumphant aria from Handel's *Messiah*. But this marvellous encouragement finds no inclusion in the new *Common Worship*, because the euphemistic liturgical processes that produced this book will certainly not mention such nasty things as worms.

There are no "vile bodies" either. What, corpses at funerals – whatever next? But because *Common Worship* avoids the stark presentation of the fact and the terror of death, the comfort and reassurance it tries to give is weakened. In *Common Worship* the Funeral Service is dislocated from the event whose terror it is meant to answer. It is therefore unreal. For example, in the *Book of Common Prayer* the "vile body" is mentioned so that in the very next line we can be reassured that at the General Resurrection God will change it "that it may be like unto his glorious body". Because the squeamish *Common Worship* omits the vileness, it is obliged to leave out the glory as well. We are offered instead "frail body". In my dictionary, "vile" is said to mean, "worthless, morally base, depraved, shameful, abject". "Frail" means only "fragile, in weak health" – just like *Common Worship's* Funeral Service in fact. Laughably, it reminds us of Monty Python's Dead Parrot sketch: he's not in weak health – he's dead.

I have discussed this issue with liturgical revisers and they say they cannot believe that the human body is vile. They do not seem to see what the vileness in question entails. It is not that there is something rotten about human flesh – though, of course, given the chance, corpses do rot; the vileness referred to in The Burial of the Dead is a moral vileness and we recall the words, "who for our sins art justly displeased".

There are moments of sheer bathos in *Common Worship's* funeral rites. There occurs the phrase,

...there is a real sense of loss at the death of a loved one.

Did even the most committed Christian believer suspect there is no such sense? There is unintentional black humour. It says,

Lord be with us as we open the door.

The mourners will laugh, surely? If only it had said, "Lord, be with us as we open the box" we could have imagined we were candidates in a macabre television quiz show.

There are prayers which contradict themselves within three lines. In one of these it says,

Although God causes grief...[then immediately goes on to say] *he does not willingly afflict or grieve anyone.*

So it looks as if God's right hand does not know what his left hand is doing. "Though worms destroy this body" has been replaced by the bizarre expression "after my skin has been destroyed" – what, through sitting too long in the sun? Further echoes of the New Age resound in a prayer which begins with the clumsy and inappropriate invocation, "Intimate God". "Reconcile us to all that we have rejected in ourselves". But this touchy-feely nonsense blinds us to the fact that there are things we ought to reject in ourselves – sin, for example. Then, "as we remember our death". As Tommy Cooper might have said, "It's a nice trick if you can do it!"

There is an order for the funeral of a child where it says, "death may be faced without fear, bitterness or guilt". Can it really be faced without fear? A few extremely brave people may come to regard death with equanimity and to stand fast against its pains; but that is not what Scripture means when it speaks of the fear of death. Death is to be feared because it is the prelude to God's judgement. Perhaps we might face death without bitterness – though the *Book of Common Prayer* offers the real meaning of the bitterness involved when it says, "Deliver us not into the bitter pains of eternal death".

The modern, therapeutic, counselling surgery style turns up again and again: "We know that, if life is soured by bitterness, an unforgiving spirit brings no peace". This is a prayer said "after a violent death". Suppose the particular violent death was the hacking to death of your wife by a mad axeman on the first day of your honeymoon – are you not allowed to feel some bitterness? The prayer after a violent death also includes the words, "It is beyond our understanding and more than we can bear". What if the case was the shooting by a soldier of a terrorist who was about to blow up a shopping arcade? This would not be beyond our understanding.

A prayer to be said "after a long illness" says, "our life is a fleeting shadow that does not endure". This fails to understand the physical and mental pains of someone who takes a long time to die: anyone enduring a prolonged agony is much more likely to feel that life is unbearably long drawn out.

Synthetic demise

The breaking down of the old local communities, the proliferation of "alternative" modern rites of passage and the growth of spurious secular counselling techniques have loosened our grip on life and so also on the way we cope with dying and death. There is more attenuation of experience away from the local and the tangible into the realm of what is increasingly official and abstract. So now our rituals of disposal make the first priority the removal of the corpse from the community in which it abode when it was animated. Gone the piano with its yellowing keys, the aspidistra and the clock and in their place the video, the stereo and the personal computer. Vile bodies do not lie easily in this new ambience, and so they are carried off to the place of euphemisms known as the Chapel of Rest and from thence to the Municipal Crematorium.

The emotional shift is profound. The aspidistra culture guaranteed that the funeral service, and in particular the words of committal, marked the parting between the living and dead. There was a continuum between the death and the disposal – a period, two or three days, during which the loss could be gradually got used to. The corpse in the front room was still one of us, part of us, part of the community. Nowadays the arrival of the undertaker with his stretcher and the removal of the corpse while it is still warm is the act of disposal. Viewings in the Chapel of Rest, and turning up a week or more later for euphemistic activity at the crematorium are kinds of embarrassed afterthoughts, willed epiphanies of religiously and socially rootless emotions.

Science and its outward and visible sign, hygiene, is god now. All our faith in science is founded: to cure us when we are ill; to replace failing parts by transplantation or gadget; to render impotence fertile and even, by techniques of resuscitation and ventilation, to redefine death itself. So when a real death comes, as it eventually must, this looks like a defeat for science. So we respond by removing the evidence – the corpse – as quickly and impersonally as possible, and our funeral rites become tributes to science – or to all that is left of science after its final failure – exercises in cleanliness and sterilization.

When Lazarus died, his friends declared "He stinketh". The Revised Standard Version of the Bible says, "There will be an odour". In the Municipal Crematorium there will not even be that. The procedure has altered. The corpse is now usually injected with embalming fluid which scientifically restores Uncle Fred's Blackpool tan without his having been forced to endure the pre-decease agony of an actual visit to that resort.

The arrangements for a crematorium are intensely bureaucratic. At least ten questions have to be answered in writing: "Are you an executor or the nearest surviving relative of the deceased? If not, state (a) your relationship to the deceased, (b) why the application is being made by you and not by an executor or any nearer relative. Have the near relatives of the deceased been informed of the proposed cremation? Has any near relative of the deceased expressed any objection to the proposed cremation? If so, on what grounds? What was the date and hour of death of the deceased? What was the place where the deceased died? Give address and say whether own residence, lodgings, hotel, hospital, nursing home, etc. Do you know, or have you any reason to suspect that the death of the deceased was due directly or indirectly to violence, poison, privation or neglect? Do you know any reason whatever for supposing that an examination of the remains of the deceased may be desirable? Give name and address of the ordinary medical attendant of the deceased. Give names and addresses of the medical practitioners who attended the deceased during his or her last illness." And so on.

The undertaker must bring to the crematorium a Certificate to Cremate. He must bring also a set of cremation forms signed by a doctor and confirmed by a second doctor who has seen the deceased within 14 days of the death. This then goes to a third doctor, the Official Medical Referee, who must also give permission. If there is any doubt at all about the circumstances of the death or the *bona fide* good wishes of the relatives, then the whole issue is referred to the Coroner who, if he is satisfied, will issue his "Certificate E".

There are conspicuous ambiguities and cultural contradictions, for the new god, science, is worshipped at the cremator. There is computer control of the furnaces and an electronic readout of the goings-on. Whistles and bleeps are likely to sound if the temperature of the cremator falls below a specified mark, or if there is too much smoke or too much pressure.

In the Code of Conduct for Cremations there is a sort of bureaucratic attempt at religious sensitivity: "The cremation of a human body is a highly emotional occasion…" Did we think it was not? They are trying to turn statements of the blindingly obvious into pseudo-religious statements, prefabricated euphemisms. The only sort of culture in which such a sleight of hand would even seem necessary is a secular and sceptical culture such as ours. The disjunction is so great that the result is bound to be only sentimental.

It is as if the authorities feel guilty about the scientific-technological ambience, and so have to offer a few pseudo-religious excuses couched in language which contrives to be at once archaic and impersonal, "…of whom may by conduct or demeanour detract from the atmosphere of reverence which it is endeavoured to create". It is a mixture of language, a sort of bureaucratic-legal-masonic.

Modern advice about death

Many new books try to teach us how to cope with dying, death and bereavement. These are mainly written in an unpalatable mixture of psychobabble, jargon and sentimentality. Consider, for example, the following extracts from *Spiritual Care of the Dying and Bereaved People* by Penelope Wilcock.[313]

> *It is the dimension of care for the dying which energises and brings meaning to the days of journeying to the eventual farewell…to allow ourselves to become a touching space and permission to people to find a truth which dignifies and heals.*

> *Be vulnerable, be sensitive, for you are on holy ground. Lay down your defences for you are on holy ground.*

This is a clumsy combination of litany style prayer and the jargon of the counselling clinic.

Whatever else a god is, it is the personification of our ideal.

This is simply not true. And what can the following mean?

Our helplessness is a gift to the helpless.

Or,

The first task of a spiritual carer is to affirm the patient's personhood and identity.

No, the first task of a carer is to care, not to indulge in suspect psychological verbiage. Some of the New Age imagery is too daft to laugh at:

Today is rainy and I have dreary chores to do, and I feel blue. But you come along, my mellow, yellow friend, and together we merge into a peaceful green... Touched by the pink of a gentle, comforting friend we may become peach.

And what about the following advice?

A carer should appear gentle and non-threatening, avoiding power-dressing and hard, boxy lines.

Elsewhere we have a mixture of the argot of the management workshop and the blindingly obvious:

Carers have to learn polite, assertive skills.

Another book, Helen Alexander's *Bereavement: A Shared Experience,* asserts the following:

The death of someone we love will be one of the most stressful and devastating events of our lives. It is a shocking and bewildering experience...it takes from us people who are part of our lives, and it removes from us people that we love.[314]

No, surely not!

There is also endless phoney psychological jargon and imagery:

A void of longing and needing is opened up and it takes time to adjust to that void.

Denial is a very common human protective mechanism.

When the subject of God is mentioned, there is only a crass ignorance of theology amounting almost to blasphemy:

While God is welcoming another of his children into a new existence, does he also recognise that those left behind are paying the price of human loving?

Or is God, too, deemed to be stupid enough to require instruction from books such as this one?

And, occasionally, complete fatuity:

If you are bereaved and also housebound and unwell, it may be that you can enjoy listening to the radio, or reading...

You might need to visit the lavatory every four hours or so as well!

On Death & Dying by Elisabeth Kubler-Ross MD contains the following obscure statement:

Depression is a tool to prepare for the impending loss of all the love objects in order to facilitate the state of acceptance.[315]

Does this mean anything at all?

Death has always been distasteful to man and probably always will be...

What is the value of "probably" here?

From a psychiatrist's point of view this is very understandable.

Do you really have to be a psychiatrist to understand that?

This book perpetuates a disagreeable psychological determinism, declaring that our response to the realisation that we are shortly to die always follows a prescribed series of mental states:

> *First stage, denial and isolation; second stage, anger; third stage, bargaining; fourth stage, depression; fifth stage, acceptance...*

Then we are offered "Therapy with the terminally ill". Why can't such a profound psychiatrist bring herself to say "dying"?

Compared with the advice and encouragement given by the words of the ancient scriptures and prayer books, the thoughts of the best poets and the most penetrating philosophers of the past, this modern jargon is depressing. It does not even approach the deep grief and bereavement which it hopes to assuage. This is not only because it is jargon but because it is produced by minds which are simply not wise enough or thoughtful enough to provide what is really needed.

When you compare Elisabeth Kubler-Ross MD with Plato or Wittgenstein or Helen Alexander with John Donne and *The Book of Common Prayer*, the contrast is stark.

The old words quoted above from many religious traditions and none, arose out of profound experience and intense thought. As there is no cheap grace, so there is no cheap wisdom either.

Notes

Chapter 1

1. And so do cohabitations.
2. C Murray, *Losing Ground*, New York: Basic Books. 1984.
3. See chapter 11, "Being ill".
4. John Donne, *Devotions Upon Emergent Occasions*, ed A Raspa, Oxford University Press, New York and Oxford, "Twenty-second meditation", pp 117-8.
5. See chapter 4, "Making and keeping friends".
6. Seneca, *Ad Lucilium Epistulae Morales*, Richard M Gummere, William Heineman, New York, 1925, Vol I, p 11.
7. Aristotle, *Ethics*, Penguin, London, 1976, p 263.
8. Translated and quoted by B McGuire, *Friendship and Community*, Cistercian Publications, Kalamazoo, 1998, p xiv.
9. See chapter 3, "Doing one's work".
10. See chapter 10, "Growing old".
11. See chapter 2, "Falling in love, getting married and staying together".
12. See chapter 5, "Raising children".
13. See chapter 9, "Punishing criminals".
14. See chapter 8, "Helping those less fortunate than ourselves".
15. Adapted from "The Ploughman and the Snake", Aesop, *The Complete Fables*, Trans Olivia and Robert Temple, Penguin, New York, 1998, Fable 82, p 65.
16. Adapted from "The Child Thief and his Mother", Aesop, *ibid*, Fable 296, p 219.
17. See chapter 6, "Playing games".
18. P G Wodehouse, *The Clicking of Cuthbert*, London 1922, p 64.
19. See chapter 7, "Appreciating the arts".

20. Matisse, *Notes d'un Peintre*, in Elizabeth Knowles (ed), The Concise Oxford Dictionary of Quotations, Oxford University Press, Oxford 2001, p 215.

21. The Bible, *Kings*, ch 20, v 1.

22. T S Eliot, "Catholicism and International Order", *Christendom*, 3, 1933, pp 171-3.

23. Maurice Cowling,, *Religion and Public Doctrine in Modern England*, Vol 3, *Accommodations*, Cambridge University Press, Cambridge, p 701.

Chapter 2

24. G Coughlan, *Boys, Girls and Sex*, Sydney: West Publishing Corporation, 1973.

25. Plato, *The Republic* (trans H D P Lee), Harmondsworth: Penguin Books, 1956, p 213.

26. B Russell, *A History of Western Philosophy*, London: Routledge, 1995, p 187.

27. Cicero, *De Officio*, Book 1, Ch 17, cited in Stevenson's Book of Quotations Classical and Modern, London: Cassell, 1950

28. Cited in A Alvarez, *Life After Marriage*, London: Fontana Paperbacks, 1982.

29. Cited in Stephenson, op cit.

30. K Blixen, *On Modern Marriage*, (trans A Born), London: Fourth Estate, 1987.

31. Ibid p 54.

32. Alvarez, op cit.

33. Cited in D Anderson, *Losing Friends*, London: Social Affairs Unit, 2001, p 191.

34. Thomas Parnell, *Hesiod*, cited in Stevenson, op cit.

35. Fosdick, *Marriage*, ibid.

36. L Hoffman, *Foundations of Family Therapy*, USA: Basic Books, 1981.

37. Colley Cibber, *Double Gallant*, cited in Stevenson, op cit.

38. Johnson, *The Rambler*, No 119, cited in Stevenson, op cit.

39. Hoffman, op cit, p 100.

40. Montaigne, *Essays*, cited in Stevenson, op cit.

41. Richard Burton, *Anatomy of Melancholy*, cited in Stevenson, op cit.

42. Menander, cited in Stevenson, op cit.

43. R L Stevenson, *Memories and Portraits*, cited in Stevenson, op cit.

44. C Kingsley, *The Saint's Tragedy*, cited in Stevenson, op cit.

45. Maria Edgeworth, *Castle Rackrent*, cited in Stevenson, op it.

46. A Pope *January and May*, cited in Stevenson, op cit.

47. O Goldsmith, *The Double Transformation*, cited in Stevenson, op cit.

48. K C Barnes, *He and She*, Harmondsworth, Penguin Books, 1968, p 173.

49. A Pope, *Eloisa to Abelard*, cited in Stevenson, op cit.

50. R L Stevenson, *Virginibus Puerisque*, cited in Stevenson, op cit.

51. Barnes, op cit. p 74.

52. Aphra Behn, *Love and Marriage*, cited in Stevenson, op cit.

53. Benjamin Franklin, *Poor Richard*, cited in Stevenson, op cit.

54. Cowley, *The Belle's Stratagem*, cited in Stevenson, op cit.

55. Wycherley, *The Country Wife*, cited in Stevenson, op cit.

56. Clarke, *Paraemiologia*, cited in Stevenson, op cit.

57. Franklin, loc cit.

58. Baum, *And Life Goes On*, cited in Stevenson, op cit.

59. Cowper, *Mutual Forbearance Necessary to the Married State*, cited in Stevenson, op cit.

60. Blixen, op cit, p 43.

61. Ibid.

62. de Maupassant, *The Love of Long Ago*, cited in Stevenson, op cit.

63. S Bean, "Soap Operas – sagas of American kinship", in W Arens and S P Montague, *The American Dimension*, Palo Alto, CA: Mayfield Pub-lishing Company, 1981.

64. Cited in Alvarez, op cit, p 126.

65. W Morris, *News from Nowhere*, cited in Alvarez, op cit, p 134.

66. B Russell, *Marriage and Morals*, London: Bantam Books, 1968.

67. A Comfort, *Sex in Society*, Harmondsworth: Penguin, 1964.

68. B Faust, Women, *Sex and Pornography*, Ringwood, Vic: Penguin Books Australia, 1980.

69. Comfort, op cit.

70. Barnes, op cit, p 81.

71. M Morgan, *The Total Woman*, cited in Faust, op cit, p 168.

72. E Jones, *Family Systems Therapy*, Chichester: John Wiley & Sons, 1993.

73. C J Sugar, "Marriage contracts", in A S Gurman and D P Kriskern (eds) *Handbook of Family Therapy*, New York: Brunner/Mazel, 1981.

74. G Corey, *Theory and Practice of Counselling and Psychotherapy*, Pacific Grove CA: Brooks-Cole, 1991

75. *Times Literary Supplement*, 25 January 2002.

76. T and N Rusk, *Mind Traps*, Harmondswoth: Harper-Collins, 1988.

77. S Jeffers, *Feel the Fear and Do It Anyway*, London, Random House, 1987.

78. S Dowrick, *Intimacy and Solitude*, Melbourne: Heinemann, 1991.

79. V Satir, *Conjoint Family Therapy*, London: Souvenir Press, 1967/1983.

80. Russell, *Love and Marriage*, op cit, p 215.

81. Coughlan, op cit, p 66.

Chapter 3

82. *Pirke Aboth*: in Charles, 693.
83. *Ecclesiastes* 8, 15.
84. *Job* 38,4 and 28-29, trans Wolfers.
85. *Isaiah* 60,21.
86. *Pirke Aboth*, Charles, 692.
87. In *Pirke Aboth*, 1962, R Travers, Herford edition 30.
88. *Ecclesiastes* 9, 10.
89. *Ecclesiastes*: Charles 417.
90. *Ecclesiastes*: Charles, 358.
91. *Proverbs* 6, 12-14.
92. *Pirke Aboth*: Charles, 701.
93. *Proverbs* 31.
94. *Proverbs* 11, 22.
95. *Pirke Aboth*: R Travers Herford, 1962.
96. *Pirke Aboth*: Charles, 713.
97. *Daily Telegraph*, 11 March 2002.
98. See his comments in *Culture and Society in Britain 1850-1890*, in J M Golby, 1988, pp 112-118.
99. *Pirke Aboth*: Charles, 695.
100. *Diary of a Nobody*, 143.
101. *Ecclesiasticus*: Charles, 412.
102. *Ecclesiasticus*: Charles, 416.

Chapter 4

103. Aristotle, *Ethics*, London: Penguin, 1976, p 263.
104. I *Samuel*, ch 20 v 17.
105. *The Times*, 6 May 2002, "Parent Forum".
106. *The Standard*, May 13, 2002.
107. Discussed in R Watters, "Coleridge, female friendship and "Lines written at Shurton Bars", *The Coleridge Bulletin*, New Series 15, Spring 2000, pp 7-8.
108. B McGuire, *Friendship and community*, Cistercian Publications, Kalamazoo, 1998, p xiv.

109. M Pahaluk et al, *Other Selves: Philosophers on friendship*, New York: Hackett, 1991.

110. Seneca, *Ad Lucilium epistulae morales*, R M Gummere, New York: William Heinemann, 1925, vol 1, p 11.

111. M de Montaigne, *Essays*, trans J M Cohen, Harmondsworth: Penguin, 1997, p 97.

112. R Lynd, *Dr Johnson and company*, Harmondsworth: Penguin, 1946.

113. St Augustine, *Confessions*, London: Penguin, IV 4 & 6.

114. J H Newman, "Love of relations and friends" in *Selected sermons, prayers and devotions: John Henry Newman*, J F Thornton and S B Varenne, New York: Vintage Books, 1998.

115. C S Lewis, *The Four Loves*, London: Fontana, 1960, p 75.

116. Ibid, p 83.

117. E M Forster, *Two cheers for democracy*, London: Edward Arnold, 1951.

118. A Sullivan, *Love undetectable*, Vintage UK, 199, pp 221-3.

119. W Shakespeare, *Julius Caesar* I ii.

120. E Burke, "Thoughts on the cause of the present discontents" in F Canavan (ed), *Selected Works of Edmund Burke vol I*, Indianapolis: Liberty Fund, 1999.

121. E Burke, "Thoughts on the cause of the present discontents", in F Canavan (ed), *Selected works of Edmund Burke vol I*, Indianapolis: Liberty Fund, 1999.

122. N Annan, *The Dons*, London: Harper Collins, 2000, p 40.

123. H Carpenter, *The Inklings*, London: Unwin, 1981.

124. L Strauss, *On Tyranny*, Chicago: University of Chicago Press, 1961.

125. Euripedes, Orestes in *Orestes*.

126. Sullivan, op cit, 176-7.

127. M Day, survey reported in *Adolescence: the importance of peer group and friendship*, PhD thesis, Brunel University, 1987.

128. D Carnegie, *How to win friends and influence people*, New York: Simon and Schuster, 1936.

129. S Duck, *Friends for life*, 2nd edn, Harvester Wheatsheaf, 1991.

130. R Bellah, *Habits of the heart*, Hutchinson, 1985, p 134.

131. G Allan, *A sociology of friendship and kinship*, London, Allen and Unwin, 1979.

132. Aristotle, op cit, Book VIII, p 261.

133. S Butler, *The way of all flesh*, London: Bestseller Library, Paul Elek Ltd, 1958, p 315.

134. C Lamb, "A bachelor's complaint" in *The complete works of Charles Lamb*, London: Chatto and Windus, 1892.

Chapter 5

135. E Burke, *Reflections on the Revolution in France,* Harmondsworth: Penguin, p 182.

136. "Sharpening the wits of mortals by cares", Virgil, *Georgics,* 1.123, Loeb, trans H Rushton Fairclough.

137. C Lasch, *Heaven in a Heartless World,* New York: Norton & Co, 1977, p 20.

138. D Kindlon PhD, *Too Much of a Good Thing,* New York: Hyperion, 2001, p 6.

139. B Cosby, from *Fatherhood,* Ch 5 (1986), quoted in S Ginsburg EdD (ed), *Family Wisdom, The 2000 Most Important Things Ever Said About Parenting Children and Family Life,* New York: Columbia University Press, 1996, p 243.

140. B Bettelheim, quoted from *A Good Enough Parent,* Ch 2, ibid, p 243.

141. L Kutner, quoted from the Introduction to *Pregnancy and Your Baby's First Year* (1993), ibid, p 246.

142. Ibid, p 247, attributed to Louise Hart, author of *The Winning Family* (1987).

143. John Gray PhD, *Children are from Heaven,* New York: Harper Collins, 1999, p 23.

144. "Taming Little Tyrants", *New York Times,* 27 May 1998.

145. *Exodus,* 20.12.

146. It may mean as Dr Laura Schlessinger writes, that "If we take care of our parents, our children will take care of us" or "the honoring of parents reinforces social order as a whole and enhances the quality of life for everyone involved." L Schlessinger, *The Ten Commandments,* New York: Harper Collins, 1998, p 147.

147. Virgil, *Aeneid;* the epithet for Aeneas is "pious Aeneas".

148. *Ecclesiasticus,* 3.11.

149. Ibid, 30.13.

150. *Proverbs,* 22.6.

151. *Proverbs,* 13.24.

152. *Proverbs,* 22.15.

153. Dr J W Varni and D G Corwin, *Time-Out for Toddlers,* New York: Berkeley Books, 1991, p 40.

154. Bullying, we found out after the Columbine shootings, is rampant in the schools nowadays.

155. Melana Zyla Vickers, "Reading, Ritalin and ' Rithmetic", *The Weekly Standard,* 11 March 2002, p 16. *The Chicago Sun Times* (21 April 2002) ran a front page article entitled "Ritalin Roulette". Their three-page story examines the inequity of the distribution of these drugs, since suburban areas far exceed

use in the inner city.

156. Gray, op cit, p 27ff.

157. Fairy tales offer "new dimensions to the child's imagination" and images "by which he can structure his daydreams and with them give better direction to his life"; B Bettelheim, *The Uses of Enchantment,* New York: Alfred Knopf, 1976, p 7.

158. Ibid, p 8.

159. "In a nutshell, RET teaches people how to live more satisfactory lives by applying logical, rational thinking." J W Maag, PhD, *Parenting without Punishment,* Philadelphia: Charles Press, 1996, p 119.

160. G Dench, *Transforming Men,* New Jersey: Transaction Publishers, 1996, see especially ch 3.

161. In *The Complete Original Edition, retold by Watty Piper,* 1986/

162. C Hoff Summers, *Who Stole Feminism?* New York: Simon and Schuster, 1994, ch 7.

163. J Derbyshire, "Excuse Me…; The Decline of Manners", *National Review Online,* 8 April 2002.

164. P D Stanhope, *The Book of Good Manners,* Santa Barbara: Bellepheron, 1993.

165. J-J Rousseau, *Discourse on the Sciences and Arts,* (First Discourse), ed R D Masters, St Martin's Press, 1964, p 36.

166. Derbyshire, op cit, p 3.

167. J Martin, "The World's Oldest Virtue", *First Things,* May 1993, pp 22-25.

168. Ibid.

169. F Hegel, *Philosophy of Right,* trans T M Knox, London: Oxford University Press, 1952, p 118.

Chapter 6

170. The Duke of Wellington legendarily attributed English victory at the Battle of Waterloo to earlier activities "on the playing fields of Eton". Presumably he would have admitted those at Harrow to a share in the glory; see Elizabeth Knowles (ed), *The Oxford Dictionary of Quotations,* 5th ed, Oxford: Oxford University Press, 1999, p 80.

171. N Gash, *Mr Secretary Peel,* London: 1961, pp 45-6.

172. Ibid, p 46.

173. Winston Churchill, *My Early Life,* London: 1930, chs 2 and 3

174. C Tyerman, *History of Harrow School,* Oxford: 2000, esp pp 338-44.

175. N Annan, *Our Age: Portrait of a Generation,* London: 1990, p 41.

176. Tyerman, op cit, p 338.
177. Churchill, op cit, ch 3.
178. P M Thornton, *Harrow School and its Surroundings*, London: 1885, ch xiv, p 337.
179. Tyerman, op cit, p 339.
180. W E Bowen, *Edward Bowen: A Memoir*, London: 1902, p 225.
181. Ibid, pp 222-5.
182. Thornton, op cit, p 331.
183. Ibid, p 340.
184. Tyerman, op cit, p 331.
185. Bowen, op cit, p 225.
186. Ibid.
187. *Harrow School: Prospectus*, 2001-2, p 9.
188. *Harrow School: Annual Information*, 2001-2, p 19.
189. Private information.
190. *Daily Telegraph*, 21 February 2002, p 9.
191. L Allison, *Amateurism in Sport*, London: 2001, p 13. Dr Allison's observations on this matter deserve the closest scrutiny.
192. Ibid, p 10.
193. Lord Mancroft, *Bees in Some Bonnets*, London: 1979, p 129.
194. P G Wodehouse, *The Clicking of Cuthbert*, London: 1922, p 64.
195. J Greaves, *The Observer*, 1 January 1989, "Saying of the Year".
196. R S Surtees, *Handley Cross*, London: 1843, p 113.
197. R Scruton, *On Hunting*, London: 1998, p 7.
198. Adam Smith, *An Enquiry into the Nature and Causes of the Wealth of Nations*, ed by R H Campbell and A S Skinner, Indianapolis: Liberty Fund, 1981, vol II, Book 5, Article 2, pp 781-2.
199. Cited in Knowles (ed), op cit, p 124.
200. Interview, ITV, in 1995.
201. S Wilde, *Letting Rip: The Fast Bowling Threat from Lillee to Waqar*, London: 1994, pp 81-2.
202. Martijn Reviser, Ipswich Town Footballer, quoted in the *Daily Telegraph*, 29 April, 2002.
203. L McKinstry, *Boycs: The True Story*, London: 2000, pp 196-202.
204. Attributed 1972; see Knowles (ed), op cit, pp 121-2.
205. Allison, op cit, p 169: "The Games were dubbed 'the first private enterprise games' and considerably strengthened the case of those who argued that sport should be run on fully commercial principles." On similar developments in cricket, see G Wright, *Betrayal: The Struggle for Cricket's Soul*, London:

1993, ch 1; and tennis, see E Digby Baltzell, *Sporting Gentlemen: Men's Tennis from the Age of Honour to the Cult of the Superstar,* New York: 1995, ch 17.

206. K S Ranjitsinghi, *The Jubilee Book of Cricket,* London: 1897, esp chs 1-5.

207. P Morrah, *The Golden Age of Cricket,* London: 1967, pp 154-5/

208. Interestingly, steel cricket bats, a fashion of the 1970s, were banned on the insistence of bowlers and fielders.

209. McKinstry, op cit, pp 214ff.

210. Allison, op cit, p 166.

211. Most recently employed in R D Putnam, *Bowling Alone: The Collapse and Revival of Community in America,* New York: 2000, see esp chs 6 and 7.

212. *The Independent,* "Education", 7 March, 2002, p 6.

213. Ibid, pp 6-7.

214. Private information. This document was shown to me on the understanding that I did not reveal the source; that was interesting in itself.

215. M Caroselli, *Great Session Openers, Closers and Energizers: Quick Activities for Warming Up Your Audience and Ending on a High Note,* New York: 1998.

216. Ibid, p 7.

Chapter 7

217. G E Lessing, *Laocoon,* ed W Steel, London: Dent, 1970 (1798) p 79.

218. R Woodfield, *The Essential Gombrich,* London: Phaidon, 1996, p 586.

219. W Pater, *The Renaissance,* Oxford: OUP, 1986, p 144.

220. E Knowles, *The Concise Oxford Dictionary of Quotations, Oxford: OUP,* 2001, p 215.

221. E Shils, "Tradition and Liberty", in S Crosby (ed) *The Virtue of Civility,* Indianapolis: Liberty Fund, 1997, p 107.

222. J J Winckelmann, in *The History of Art and Antiquity* (1764) quoted in A Potts, *Flesh and the Ideal: Winckelmann and the Origins of Art History,* New Haven: Yale University Press, 1994, p 54.

223. Shils, op cit, p 586

224. Woodfield, op cit, p 586.

225. Andre Malraux in *Les Voix du Silence* (1951, pt 4, ch 7), quoted in Woodfield, op cit, p 588.

226. Goethe, quoted in Woodfield, op cit, p 588.

227. C Leigh, "Teaching Tradition", *The American Enterprise,* January/February 2002, p 39.

228. Woodfield, op cit, p 585.

229. J Gage, *Goethe on Art*, London: Scolar Press, 1980.

230. J Bayley, *Iris*, London: Abacus, 2002, pp 129-30.

231. Lessing, op cit, p 9.

232. M-H Wood (ed) *Edvard Munch: the Frieze of Life*, London: The National Gallery, 1992, p 12.

233. Newbolt Committee *The Teaching of English in England, 1921,* quoted in J Giles T Middleton (eds*), Writing Englishness 1900-1950,*,London: Routledge, 1995, p 157.

234. N Pevsner, *The Englishness of English Art*, London: Penguin, (1956) 1988; R Scruton, *England: An Elegy*, London: Pimlico, 2000.

235. N Pevsner, op cit, pp 200-1.

236. W Pater on the changes in William Morris' poetry, quoted in A S Leoussi, *Nationalism and Classicism*, Houndmills: Macmillan, 1998, p 101.

Chapter 8

237. *Deuteronomy*, XV, 4,5.

238. *Deuteronomy*, XV, 11.

239. Maimonides, *Laws of Gifts to the Poor*, ch 7, section 5.

Chapter 9

240. *Leviticus* 24, 17-22.

241. Adapted from Aesop, "The Fox with the Swollen Stomach", *The Complete Fables*, trans O and R Temple, NY: Penguin, 1998, Fable 30 p 26.

242. Adapted from "The Ploughman and the Frozen Snake, Aesop, op cit, Fable 82, p 65.

243. Nietzsche, *Dawn*, section 202 in R Solomon and M Murphy, *What is Justice?* New York: Oxford, 2nd edn, 2000.

244. Nietzsche, *Zarathrustra* 11, ibid.

245. *Matthew*, 5, 38-42.

246. Raskolnikov speaks of his intended murder in F Dostoyevsky, *Crime and Punishment,* trans S Monas, Signet Classic, 1968, p 73.

247. "Town Rat and Country Rat", from Jean de la Fontaine, *The Best Fables of La Fontaine*, trans F Duke, Charlottesville: University Press of Virginia, p12.

248. A Burgess, *A Clockwork Orange*, NY: Ballantine, 1963, p 96, Prison Chaplain

to Alex.

249. "The Two Mules", de la Fontaine, op cit, p 6.
250. Adapted from "The Child Thief and his Mother", Aesop, op cit, Fable 296, p 219.

Chapter 10

251. *The Dialogues of Plato*, trans B Jowett, Vol II, Oxford: Clarendon Press, 1871.
252. *Letters of Marcus Tullius Cicero, with his Treatises on Friendship and Old Age*, trans E S Shuckburgh, The Harvard Classics, Vol IX, New York: P F Collier, 1909.
253. From "An Acre of Grass", *Collected Poems of W B Yeats*, London: Macmillan, 1961.
254. "Sailing to Byzantium", second stanza, loc cit.
255. "Among School Children", first stanza, loc cit.
256. Ibid, fourth stanza.
257. Philip Larkin "The Old Fools", first stanza, *Collected Poems*, ed and introd A Thwaite, London: Marvell Press and Faber and Faber, 1988.
258. Ibid, second stanza.
259. "Aubade", opening stanzas, loc cit.
260. Wordsworth, *Poetry and Prose*, selected by W M Merchant, London: Rupert Hart-Davis, 1955.

Chapter 11

261. N C Smith (ed), *Selected Letters of Sydney Smith*, Oxford: Oxford University Press, 1981, p 231.
262. E Waugh, *Brideshead Revisited*, Penguin edition, p 316.
263. *2 Kings*, 20:1.
264. *All's Well That Ends Well*, II.ii.113-23.
265. J Donne, *Devotions Upon Emergent Occasions*, ed A Raspa, New York and Oxford: Oxford University Press, 1987, "Twenty-second Meditation", pp 117-8.
266. Ed cit, p 7.
267. Ed cit, p 22.
268. Ed cit, pp 23-25.
269. Ed cit, p 34.

270. J Boswell, *The Life of Samuel Johnson*, ed C Rawson, London: Everyman's Library, 1992, pp 115-16.

271. H Tennyson, *Alfred Lord Tennyson: A Memoir by His Son*, 2 vols, London: Macmillan, 1897, ii 350-52.

272. J Thurber, *The Secret Life of Walter Mitty and Other Pieces*, Penguin edition, pp 70-71.

273. T S Eliot, "Catholicism and international order", *Christendom* 3, 1933, pp 172-73.

Chapter 12

274. *Psalms* 23: 1-4.

275. *Job* 19: 25-27.

276. *St John* 3: 16.

277. *St John* 11: 25-26.

278. *St John* 14: 1-3.

279. *Romans* 8: 35-39.

280. *I Corinthians* 15: 19-22.

281. *I Corinthians* 15: 35-57.

282. *I Thessalonians* 4: 13-18.

283. *The Revelation of St John the Divine* 21: 1-4.

284. The Burial of the Dead, *Book of Common Prayer*, 1662.

285. At the Burial, *First Prayer Book of Edward VI*, 1549.

286. The Burial of the Dead, op cit.

287. ibid.

288. Roman Catholic Liturgy of the Dead, *The Daily Missal*.

289. Ibid.

290. In Paradisum, ibid.

291. J W Goethe, *Conversations with Eckermanm*, 1828.

292. Epicurus (341-27BC), Letter to Menoeceus.

293. L Wittgenstein (1889-1951), *Tractatus Logico Philosophicus*.

294. Lucretius (94-55BC) *De Rerum Natura*.

295. Artur Schopenauer (1788-1869), *The Indestructibility of Being*.

296. Jeremy Taylor (1613-67), *Holy Dying*.

297. William Hazlitt (1778-1830), *On the Fear of Death*.

298. John Donne (1572-1631), "Death Be Not Proud", *Holy Sonnets*.

299. Jonathan Swift (1667-1745), *Thoughts on Religion*.

300. C G Jung (1875-1961), *The Soul and Death*.

301. Gitanjali (1861-1941), *Rabindranath Tagore.*

302. Lyall Wilkes (b 1914), *Nightmare.*

303. Swift, *Gulliver's Travels.*

304. C P Cavaty (1863-1933), *Lovely White Flowers.*

305. C S Lewis (1898-1963), *A Grief Observed.*

306. Joyce Grenfell (1910-1979), *Joyce: By Herself and Her Friends.*

307. Edmund Burke (1729-1797), Letter to Matthew Smith.

308. Christina Rossetti (1830-94), *Time Flies.*

309. Martin Frayn (b 1933), *Constructions.*

310. Blaise Pascal, *Pensees.*

311. Saul Bellow (b 1915), *Humboldt's Gift.*

312. Samuel Johnson quoted in James Boswell, *Life of Johnson*, 1791.

313. P Wilcock, *Spiritual Care of the Dying and Bereaved People*, London: SPCK, 1996.

314. H Alexander, *Bereavement: A Shared Experience*, Oxford: Lion, 1993.

315. E Kubler-Ross, *On Death & Dying*, New York: Simon & Schuster, 1997.

Some Publications from the Social Affairs Unit

GENTILITY RECALLED
"MERE" MANNERS AND THE MAKING OF SOCIAL ORDER

Edited by Digby Anderson

Published in association with THE ACTON INSTITUTE

"I wanted to know why the world had changed so much
and I got the answer from *Gentility Recalled*"
Bernard Levin in *The Times*

THE LOSS OF VIRTUE
MORAL CONFUSION AND SOCIAL DISORDER
IN BRITAIN AND AMERICA

Edited by Digby Anderson

A NATIONAL REVIEW book

"…cogent, brave and timely…"
Catholic Herald

THIS WILL HURT
THE RESTORATION OF VIRTUE & CIVIC ORDER

Edited by Digby Anderson

A NATIONAL REVIEW book

Cutting crime and restoring order and virtue cannot be done without costs.
It requires the re-learning of social sanctions, ways of making people good.
It will hurt.

LOSING FRIENDS

Digby Anderson

"A Tour de Force"
National Review

FAKING IT:
THE SENTIMENTALISATION
OF MODERN SOCIETY

Edited by Digby Anderson & Peter Mullen

"The more people who read this book the better"
Chris Woodhead *Sunday Telegraph*

LOYALTY MISPLACED
MISDIRECTED VIRTUE AND SOCIAL DISINTEGRATION

Edited by Gerald Frost

THE DICTIONARY OF DANGEROUS WORDS

Compiled by Digby Anderson

"This book will shortly replace a university education. And it's cheaper"
John Cleese

COME BACK MISS NIGHTINGALE
TRENDS IN PROFESSIONS TODAY

Edited by Digby Anderson

The professions are threatened by anti-elitism, the cult of informality, managerialism and the loss of collegiality: above all, by the elevation of expertise over character.

MARKETING THE REVOLUTION

THE NEW ANTI-CAPITALISM
AND THE ATTACK UPON CORPORATE BRANDS

Michael Mosbacher

How seriously should the new critics of capitalism be treated?
A good number are doing little that is new. Even their emphasis on
individual alleged abuses is, at least in part, not a new end
but a means to galvanize support for their hatred of capitalism.

CALLED TO ACCOUNT:

THE CASE FOR AN AUDIT OF THE STATE
OF THE FAILING CHURCH OF ENGLAND

Edited by Digby Anderson

The Church of England's love-affair with modernity has been unrequited.
The liberal experiment is dead. Unfortunately, it is in danger of taking the
Church into the grave with it.

ANOTHER COUNTRY

Edited by Michael Mosbacher & Digby Anderson

Country people are used to being an ignored minority.
Today, urbanites, especially policy-makers, while still ignorant about
country life, no longer ignore it. They patronise and interfere with it. This
attack on country livelihoods, pleasures and culture comes from four
groups: activists, sentimentalists, modernisers and regulators.
Their ignorant interference, if successful, will destroy the countryside.
In *Another Country*, academics, journalists, farmers but, most importantly,
people engaged in country livelihoods and culture, correct myths behind
the urbanites' assault.